Pressure Cooker Magic

101 Fast and Fabulous Recipes for Your Electric Pressure Cooker

Alison DuBois Scutte

Good Books®

New York, New York

PRESSURE COOKER MAGIC

Copyright © 2017 by Alison DuBois Scutte

Good Books books may be purchased in bulk at special discounts for sales promotion, corporate gifts, fund-raising, or educational purposes. Special editions can also be created to specifications. For details, contact the Special Sales Department, Good Books, 307 West 36th Street, 11th Floor, New York, NY 10018 or info@skyhorsepublishing.com.

Good Books is an imprint of Skyhorse Publishing, Inc.®, a Delaware corporation.

Visit our website at www.goodbooks.com.

10 9 8 7 6 5 4 3 2

Library of Congress Cataloging-in-Publication Data available on file.

ISBN: 978-1-68099-216-8
eBook ISBN: 978-1-68099-217-5

Cover design by Jane Sheppard
Cover photo by Bonnie Matthews
Interior photos by Bonnie Matthews

Printed in China

Contents

Beyond the Manual
Tips & Tricks to Master Your Electric Pressure Cooker

Let's Get Cooking
Recipes, Tips & Time Charts

A Note from the Author

My motivation for writing this book was to help the tens of thousands of you who have purchased electric pressure cookers after watching TV shopping presentations and info-mercials, only to be disappointed once you started using it. If you were using an older pressure cooker cookbook, it's no wonder your foods never seemed to be cooked as well as the food looked on TV! It's not your fault, and it's not the pressure cooker's fault . . . it's the book you are using!

Most cookbooks written for pressure cookers are actually written for stove-top cookers, not electric. Does it make a difference? Absolutely! Stove-top versions can cook foods at 15 PSI, while the majority of electric versions max out at 12 PSI. That makes a huge difference when it comes to cooking times. Now that you have the right book, you should have better results.

In fact, the actual recipes that are used in many of the presentations on shopping channels and infomercials can be found right here in this book!

Thank you!

Thanks to my husband Al for his encouragement, for roughing it on his own while I was glued to my computer for the last few months, and for his superb photography skills! Thanks also to Katie for giving me the push I needed to finally write this book! Finally, my special thanks goes out to all of you TV shoppers who continue to write and share your cooking experiences (good and bad) with me. It keeps me on my "culinary toes," helps me continue to develop new recipes and WOW demos for on-air presentations, and warms my heart to hear that some of my recipes have woven their way into the fabric of your family. I hope that these new recipes bring much joy to your family dinner table for years to come, and I look forward to hearing more of your stories!

Happy Cooking!

—Alison D. Scutte

Beyond the Manual
Tips & Tricks to Master
Your Electric Pressure Cooker

Wouldn't it be nice if product manuals gave you the inside skinny on using a pressure cooker?!

I'm not saying that the manual included with your cooker isn't loaded with information necessary for you to use the appliance correctly. It absolutely is, but . . . there are many little nuances and tips that will minimize the fallout meals during the learning curve! That's where my book comes in!

As a child, I watched my grandmother and mother use pressure cookers and enjoyed the delicious meals. Now, as an adult, I have worked professionally with pressure cookers for over seventeen years and learned many tricks and time-saving techniques along the way. Most of my work with pressure cookers comes from writing and presenting demonstrations on live TV, so timing and appearance is always important.

The next few pages are loaded with information that will give you a great foundation to create fabulous meals in less time than you can imagine. However, if you only take away these three rules of thumb about electric pressure cooking, you will save yourself time, frustration, and messy cabinets!

Be Prepared

The French have a phrase: *mise en place*, which loosely means "everything prepped, ready, and in its place." This is the most important habit you should adopt when using your electric pressure cooker. I cannot stress how important it is to have everything ready *before* you plug in your pressure cooker! The cooker gets hot quickly and will burn your first ingredients if you're rushing to measure liquid and seasonings. It takes much less time in the long run if you just go ahead and prepare/measure all of the veggies, meats, liquids, and seasonings before you begin to cook.

Wait for the Pressure

After attaching the lid and setting the pressure regulator, remain in close proximity until pressure has been reached. Sometimes it is necessary to jiggle the exhaust valve or twist the lid to help the cooker achieve a proper seal. If you leave and pressure is never achieved, your food will be undercooked and/or burned.

Use a Paper Towel when Exhausting Pressure

At no time should you restrict the air flow from the regulator when releasing the steam, but there is nothing wrong with lightly draping a paper towel across the pressure regulator before exhausting the pressure to catch that first oily steam containing food particles. It's an easy step that you will be very glad you remembered!

These three tips will go a long way in helping you master electric pressure cooking, but there is much more to know!

Pressure Cooking Basics

Always review your manufacturer's instruction manual prior to using your electric pressure cooker for the first time. It is very important to feel comfortable with your appliance and to be familiar with all of its special features. Each individual cooker will have specific directions for bringing food up to pressure and releasing the pressure after the cooking time has elapsed; it is imperative that you follow the directions to ensure safe cooking.

If you misplace the manual, contact the manufacturer for a replacement. Most manufacturers offer manuals (as well as recipes) in downloadable files on their websites, so take advantage of the service for worry-free cooking. If you are using an older model and are unsure of the safety features, try to contact the manufacturer or ask your local librarian for a pressure cooker cookbook that was published in approximately the same year the cooker was manufactured. If you cannot get a manual or instructions for safe usage, *do not use the cooker!*

Adapting Your Favorite Recipes

Everyone has their favorite recipes. Luckily, many can be adapted for use in your pressure cooker by following the rules and tips below, along with the time charts, listed within each chapter of this book.

- Recipes developed for slow cookers, rice cookers, and stove-top methods usually work well in a pressure cooker. However, recipes prepared by frying, grilling, or baking do not generally yield positive results.
- Separate foods to be cooked according to size and length of cooking time needed. Many recipes will require that cooking be interrupted and additional fruits and vegetables be added at a later time. Refer to the time charts so that all ingredients are cooked to their perfect level of doneness.

- Allow a minimum of ½ cup of liquid for every 10 minutes of cooking time. If time exceeds 30 minutes, add an additional ½ cup liquid to the recipe. Liquids may be water, juice, stock, broth, tomato sauce, and purees—but *not* oil.
- Never use less liquid than directed by your cooker's manual.
- Allow a minimum of 1 cup of liquid per 10 minutes of steaming time for vegetables and seafood.
- Decrease the amount of seasonings by a quarter as pressure cooking retains more of a given food's natural flavor and seasonings are infused into the foods. Taste the food after cooking and add additional seasoning if needed next time you make the recipe.
- Refer to the chapters in this cookbook for some general rules and tips specific to various foods. These guidelines will help you adapt recipes for meats and poultry, seafood, soups, vegetables, rice, grains, and desserts.

To adapt the cooking time from traditional stove-top or oven methods to pressure cooking, you must be aware of the PSI of your pressure cooker. Consult your manual to find this information and then adjust your cooking times as follows:

- If using low pressure (5–8 PSI), reduce stated cooking time by a quarter.
- If using medium pressure (10–12 PSI), reduce stated cooking time by a third.
- If using high pressure (13–15 PSI), reduce stated cooking time by half.

You can always add cooking time if needed, but you can't uncook overcooked foods! In general, I suggest you start by reducing the time by a third, checking for doneness, and then cooking longer if needed.

Browning and Searing Directions

Most recipes will instruct you to brown the foods first. Although optional, this step will not only enhance the flavor, but will also yield a more attractive finished dish. To brown the food directly in the pressure cooker:
- Heat your electric pressure cooker by selecting the preprogrammed Brown button or simply add 7 minutes to the Cook Time (7 minutes is usually enough time to brown any of your foods, but you can set it for longer if needed).
- Preheat a tablespoon or two of oil before adding food to the pot.
- Turn the foods often to ensure even browning on all sides. When browning is complete, remove large cuts of meat and immediately add a little (about ¼ cup) liquid and loosen the stuck-on bits by scraping the bottom of the pan with a spatula or spoon. Not only will this greatly improve the richness of the flavor, it will keep any burning

to a minimum during the cooking process. Replace the meat or add the remaining ingredients.

- Remember to press Cancel before setting the actual pressure cooking time needed for your recipe.

Steaming and Roasting Directions

- When cooking fresh vegetables or large cuts of meat in your pressure cooker, it is preferable to use a rack, trivet, or steamer basket to keep the food off of the bottom of the pan.
- If cooking whole or chopped fresh vegetables, pour the desired liquid into the cooker first and then load the vegetables into the steamer basket (or oven-safe dish) before lowering it into the cooker.
- If using a large cut of meat, follow the steps given in Browning and Searing Directions (starting on page 3). After you have deglazed the pan by adding your liquid, place a trivet or basket into the bottom of the cooker and position the meat on top. Add the remaining ingredients and continue to the next step in the recipe.
- If your pressure cooker did not come with a trivet or rack, you may buy a fold-out steamer basket at any cooking store or use jar lids or rings distributed around the bottom of your cooker!

How to Load the Ingredients

Never exceed the fill line of your pressure cooker. The cooker needs space to generate the necessary steam to promote pressure. Your cooker has been designed and tested to rapidly produce pressure with an allotted capacity. Never overload your cooker!

How to Position the Lid

Attach and lock the lid onto the bottom of the cooker by following the directions for your specific cooker. However, before you position the lid, it is best to always perform the following inspections to ensure the fastest, safest cooking:

- Check that the gasket is clean and inserted correctly into the lid. If the gasket seems dry, remove it from the lid, use mineral oil to lubricate it, and then replace into its proper position as directed in your cooker's manual.

- Inspect the exhaust valve to be sure there are no obstructions. Most cookers come with a tool for clearing the exhaust valve, but if yours did not, use a **metal** skewer to ensure the opening is free of debris. Never use a wooden skewer or toothpick as it may break off in the valve opening!
- Adding 1 tablespoon oil to the liquid in the cooker will help the gasket stay lubricated and the exhaust valve clear.

How to Use the Condensation Cup

This is a handy feature that keeps moisture from leaking onto your countertop while cooking! If your pressure cooker came with a condensation cup, be sure it is in place before bringing the cooker up to pressure. Consult your manual for instructions on how to correctly attach the cup.

How to Bring the Cooker up to Pressure

Since you are using an electric pressure cooker, all you need to do is: set the exhaust valve to the Air Tight (or closed) position, select your Cook Time or preprogrammed time, and press Start! Most electric cookers will automatically bring the cooker to pressure and then regulate it to keep the pressure at a steady level. A few extra tips:

- If the pressure cooker is hissing or if any steam is escaping, it is *not* under full pressure. Jiggle the exhaust valve until it is silent with no steam. If that doesn't help, you should remove the lid and check that the gasket is in place.
- Most electric pressure cookers use a medium pressure (about 12 PSI) and cannot be adjusted. If you are using a recipe that calls for low or high pressure, please read about adapting your recipe on pages 2–3.

How to Release the Steam

When cooking is complete, press Cancel or unplug the cooker. The lid cannot be removed until the pressure is released. The steam should be released according to the manufacturer's directions and the type of food being cooked (see the time charts in the related chapter of this cookbook for suggested release methods). There are three general methods to releasing the steam:

Quick Release Method

- Push, turn, or press the release valve into the open position. You may do this in bursts or in one continual motion, but **be careful** as the steam is very hot!
- Quick releasing usually takes 30–45 seconds and can be useful for recipes that may overcook or need to have other ingredients added. However, there are foods like rice, grains, and beans that should *never* be quick-released; rather, they work well with the Cold Water Release Method (below).
- Although you do *not* want to block the steam as it is being released, I hold a paper towel loosely over the vent. This captures the oils and food particles that may be expelled during steam release.

Cold Water Release Method

- Place the cooker in the sink (be sure the cooker is unplugged!) under a stream of cold running water. This works well for foods that have a lot of foam (such as rice, grains, and beans) as well as for soups and other foods that contain mostly liquid.
- Once the pressure indicator drops to "normal," the cooker can be removed from the sink and opened. This method usually takes 4–5 minutes.

Natural Release Method

- As the name indicates, this method allows the cooker to cool at its own pace and release the steam naturally. You can however, help it along by placing the cooker away from heat and laying a damp towel over it.
- Make sure that the electric cooker does not automatically go to the "Keep Warm" setting, or this process will take much longer! If it does, press Cancel.
- This is the ideal method for rice, large cuts of meat, cheesecakes, and desserts, as well as stews and other dishes that benefit from longer cooking times.
- This method takes anywhere from 5–15 minutes depending on the amount of food inside of the cooker.

NOTE: If you have released the pressure but the lid will not open, it means that the cooker is under a vapor lock or vacuum lock. If this happens, unlock the lid, turn the exhaust valve to the open position, and bring the cooker back to a low, nonpressurized heat for a couple of minutes. The lid should then come off easily.

SAFETY TIP
Always open the lid *away* from your face!

Cleaning and Maintaining
Your Pressure Cooker

Keeping your pressure cooker clean and maintained is instrumental to safe cooking and will extend the life of your cooker, so you will have years of problem-free cooking. Here are a few instructions and tips:

- Never put your pressure cooker lid in the dishwasher! Hand wash only and dry thoroughly before storing.
- Remove the insert from electric pressure cookers, wash and dry thoroughly, and wipe inside the cooker with a damp cloth before reinserting the removable pot.
- Empty, wash, and dry the condensation cup (if applicable). Store inside cooker to prevent it from being knocked off or lost in between uses.
- Store accessories, manuals, and plugs inside the cooker so they are not misplaced.
- Store the unit with the lid inverted, not in the locked position. This will prevent odors from being trapped inside the cooker.
- Always check that the gasket is clean and inserted correctly into the lid. If the gasket seems dry, remove it from the lid, use mineral oil to lubricate it, and then replace it into the proper position as directed in your cooker's manual. Properly maintained, the gasket should last about 150 uses.
- Before and after each use, inspect the exhaust valve to be sure there are no obstructions. Some lids have a snap-on screen on the inside of the lid to prevent clogs. Be sure to remove this to clean the exhaust valve. Most cookers come with a tool for clearing the exhaust valve, but if yours did not, use a metal skewer to ensure the opening is free of debris. Do **not** use a wooden skewer or toothpick as it may break off inside the valve.
- Never place the lid on a hot stove or over a burner as it may damage the gasket. If the gasket is holding odors, soak it in hot white vinegar for 5–10 minutes. Remove, wash as usual, dry, and replace inside the lid. Remember to oil it before its next use.

Let's Get Cooking!

Recipes, Tips & Time Charts

Soups & Chilis

Soups & Chilis

SLOW COOK FAST!

Soups, stews, and chili usually require all-day slow cooking for rich, flavorful results. By using your pressure cooker, you will get the same slow-cooked flavors in a fraction of the time. Try a few of the recipes in this chapter, and you'll be hooked!

Tips for Cooking Soups & Stocks

- Soups with ingredients that tend to foam, like dried beans and split peas, could cause the exhaust valve to clog. To prevent this, add 1 tablespoon of oil to each cup of dried beans or other foam-inducing ingredients.
- Due to the lack of evaporation caused by a pressure cooker, reduce the liquid required in standard recipes by 1 cup. Reduce the liquid further if necessary to remain BELOW the "max fill line" of your pressure cooker!
- Soups will take approximately 20 minutes to come to pressure due to the large liquid ratio.
- Refer to the time chart when making soups containing mixtures of meats, beans, and vegetables. The vegetables will overcook if added at the same time as the meat!
- Season lightly as pressure cookers intensify the flavors. You can adjust later if necessary.
- Release pressure using the Natural Release Method or the Cold Water Method only.

Great Northern Bean Soup

Prep Time: 70 min   **Ready in:** 45 min   **Yield:** 6–8 servings

INGREDIENTS

16 ounces dried great northern beans
10 cups water
2 tablespoons oil
8 ounces ham cubes
7 cups water
1 small onion, chopped
1 cup celery ribs and leaves, sliced
1 cup carrots, chopped
2 bay leaves
1 teaspoon coarse ground black
    pepper
2 teaspoons kosher salt
3 dashes Tabasco®
1 cup instant mashed potato flakes

COOK'S TIP

If a thicker soup
is desired, add an
additional ½ cup
potato flakes.

1. Place your pressure cooker on a level surface and plug the unit in.

2. Add dried beans and 10 cups water into pressure pan. Set Cook Time to 4 minutes and press Start.

3. Attach and lock the lid of your pressure cooker; set the pressure control to Air Tight (closed). When cooking is complete, press Cancel to turn off the Keep Warm feature and let rest 1 hour.

4. Remove lid; drain and rinse beans. Leave in the colander until needed.

5. Wash and dry the pan and place back into the base. Set Cook Time for 30 minutes and press Start.

6. Add oil and, when hot, add ham cubes and brown lightly for about 1 minute.

7. Add 7 cups water and scrape the bottom of the pan with a spatula to loosen any ham bits. Add the rinsed beans and the remaining ingredients, except for potato flakes, and stir well.

8. Replace lid, close the exhaust valve, and let cook for the rest of the 30-minute period.

9. When cooking time has elapsed, press Cancel to turn off the Keep Warm setting and let pressure release naturally until you can safely remove lid.

10. Check to make sure that the beans are tender; if not, replace lid and cook another 10 minutes.

11. When beans are tender, stir in the potato flakes.

12. Cover with glass lid (or pressure cooker lid with valve on Exhaust) and allow to cook on low 5 minutes. Remove bay leaves before serving.

Split Pea & Ham Soup

Prep Time: 70 min   **Ready in:** 45 min   **Yield:** 6 0 servings

INGREDIENTS

1 pound green split peas, rinsed and
   picked clean
2 tablespoons oil
2 large smoked ham hocks, diced
1 small onion, chopped
1 cup celery ribs and leaves, sliced
1 cup carrots, chopped
4 sprigs fresh thyme
1 bay leaf
6 cups low-sodium chicken broth
   or stock, water, or a combination
   of both
Kosher salt and freshly ground black
   pepper

COOK'S TIP
If a thicker soup
is desired, add an
additional ½ cup
potato flakes.

1. Place your pressure cooker on a level surface and plug the unit in.

2. Drain and rinse peas. Leave in the colander until needed.

3. Set Cook Time for 30 minutes and press Start.

4. Add oil; when oil is hot, add diced ham and brown lightly for about 1 minute.

5. Add the water and scrape the bottom of the pan with a spatula to loosen any ham bits. Add the rinsed peas and the remaining ingredients.

6. Attach lid, close the exhaust valve to Air Tight (closed), and let cook for the rest of the 30-minute period.

7. When cooking time has elapsed, cancel the Keep Warm setting and let pressure release naturally until you can safely remove lid. Remove bay leaf and thyme stems and discard.

8. Check to make sure that the beans are tender; if not, replace lid and cook another 10 minutes.

9. Remove ½ cup of the split peas and mash them in a blender or food processor. Stir back into the soup.

10. Cover with glass lid (or pressure cooker lid with valve on Exhaust) and allow to cook on low 5 minutes.

Ultimate Chili with Meat & Beans

Prep Time: 15 min **Ready in:** 45 min **Yield:** 10-12 servings

INGREDIENTS
1 tablespoon vegetable oil
1 ¼ pounds ground turkey
1 pound ground beef (at least
    80% lean)
1 medium onion chopped
    (about 1 cup)
1 medium green bell pepper coarsely
    chopped (about 1 cup)
½ teaspoon garlic powder
3 teaspoons ground cumin
1 teaspoon salt
3 tablespoons chili powder
1 29-ounce can crushed tomatoes
1 29-ounce can tomato sauce
1 ½ cups water, divided
1 cup V-8® juice (spicy flavor)
1 pound dried kidney beans, rinsed
    and picked clean

COOK'S TIP
You may use all turkey
or all beef if desired.

1. Place pressure cooker on a level surface, insert the pan, and plug in the unit.

2. Set Cook Time for 35 minutes and press Start.

3. Add the oil, ground turkey, and ground beef to pan. Begin browning the meat, stirring often. When meat begins to brown, stir in the chopped onion and pepper along with the garlic powder, cumin, salt, and chili powder. Stir and cook about 1 minute.

4. Stir in the crushed tomatoes and the tomato sauce. Pour ¾ cup water into each can and swish around to capture the remaining tomato and then pour into the pot.

5. Add the spicy V-8 juice and the kidney beans.

6. Attach the lid and set regulator valve to Air Tight (closed).

7. When cooking time has elapsed, unplug the pressure cooker and let the pressure release naturally.

8. Carefully open the lid, stir, and taste the beans for doneness. If more time is needed, set the pressure cooker to Keep Warm and simmer until done. Cover with the pressure lid (with valve on Exhaust) or with the glass lid.

Dress Up Your Chili!

Chili is a favorite pressure cooker recipe because you can make it with dried beans. Not only a healthy and delicious choice, but a very cost effective way to serve a large group!

To keep it interesting, think outside the bowl and serve your chili over . . .

tortilla chips

hot baked potatoes

hot dogs

southwestern salads

elbow macaroni

Fritos® corn chips

And top it with . . .

shredded cheese

sour cream

diced onions

sliced jalapeño pepper

White Chili

Prep Time: 15 min **Ready in:** 40 min **Yield:** 8–10 servings

INGREDIENTS
2 pounds boneless skinless chicken
   breast
1 tablespoon olive oil
2 large onions, chopped
5 cloves garlic, chopped
¼ cup lime juice
1 teaspoon lime zest
red pepper flakes
2 16-ounce cans great northern beans
1 4-ounce can green chilies
1 tablespoon cumin
1 teaspoon salt
1–2 teaspoons cayenne pepper
   depending on heat desired
3–4 cups chicken broth
finely shredded Monterey Jack or
   cheddar cheese (optional)
sour cream (optional)

COOK'S TIP
To make this chili using dried beans, just add 1 cup liquid and increase the cooking time to 40 minutes!

1. Place your pressure cooker on a level surface and plug the unit in.

2. Set Cook Time to 20 minutes or select the Chicken setting; press Start.

3. When the pot is hot, add the oil. Add the chicken pieces and cook until they are beginning to brown.

4. Stir in the onions and cook until they are soft. Add garlic, lime juice, lime zest, and a generous pinch of crushed red peppers.

5. Add the beans, chilies, cumin, salt, and cayenne (if desired); stir well. Add your desired amount of chicken stock based on your preferred thickness of the chili.

6. Attach the lid and set the pressure valve to Air Tight (closed).

7. When the cooking time has elapsed, press Cancel to turn off the Keep Warm setting and allow cooker to sit 10 minutes before manually releasing the remaining pressure. Carefully open the lid away from you and stir the chili well.

8. Serve with shredded Monterey Jack or cheddar cheese and a dollop of sour cream for an extra-yummy treat!

Chicken Tortilla Soup

Prep Time: 15 min **Ready in:** 35 min **Yield:** 6–8 servings

INGREDIENTS

1 store-bought rotisserie chicken, or
the meat from 1 3-pound cooked
chicken
2 tablespoons olive oil
½ cup sweet yellow onion, chopped
½ cup crushed tortilla chips
1 15¼-ounce can whole kernel corn,
drained
1½ teaspoons ground cumin
1 4-ounce can chopped green chilies
1 15½-ounce can black beans, top
liquid drained
1 28-ounce can crushed tomatoes
6 cups chicken broth
2 tablespoons chicken base (Better
Than Bouillon® chicken base
recommended)
1 small pinch dried chipotle chili
pepper
sour cream, avocado, and tortilla
chips as desired

COOK'S TIP
You can use boneless, skinless
chicken breast to eliminate the
boning process. After cooking, cut
or shred the breasts, add to the
broth with the veggies, and continue
as directed.

1. Remove the meat from the rotisserie chicken; discard bones and skin. Chop meat into bite-sized pieces. Set aside.

2. Place your pressure cooker on a level surface and plug the unit in.

3. Set Cook Time to 20 minutes or select the Soup/Stew setting; press Start.

4. Add the olive oil and chopped onion to the pot and sauté for about 2 minutes, stirring often. Add the crushed corn chips and cook another minute. Add the corn and cumin and cook another minute.

5. Add the chopped chicken and remaining ingredients—except sour cream, avocado, and tortilla chips—stirring after each ingredient.

6. Attach the lid and set the pressure valve to Air Tight (closed).

7. When cooking time has elapsed, cancel the Keep Warm feature and allow the pressure to release naturally.

8. To serve: Ladle the soup into a bowl. Top with a dollop of sour cream, avocado pieces, and crumbled tortilla chips if desired.

Oktoberfest Beer Cheese Soup

Prep Time: 15 min   **Ready in:** 30 min   **Yield:** 8–10 servings

INGREDIENTS

1 stick butter (½ cup)
1 medium sweet yellow onion,
    minced (about 1 cup)
1 medium carrot, finely diced
    (about 1 cup)
2 stalks celery, finely diced
    (about ½ cup)
½ teaspoon celery salt
½ teaspoon paprika
½ teaspoon dry mustard
½ teaspoon salt
⅓ cup + 2 tablespoons flour
1 bottle dark beer (Samuel Adams®
    Oktoberfest recommended)
5 cups chicken broth
12 ounces sharp cheddar cheese,
    shredded
4 ounces cream cheese, cut into pieces
½ teaspoon Tabasco®
1 cup half-and-half

EVERYONE LOVES BEER CHEESE FONDUE!

To make this recipe as a dip, reduce
the amount of flour to just ½ cup
and the chicken broth to just 3
cups. To serve, offer alongside
hard pretzel sticks, garlic croutons,
carrots, sliced green apples, and
cauliflower and broccoli florets.

1. Place your pressure cooker on a level surface and plug the unit in. Set Cook Time to 20 minutes; press Start.

2. Add the cold butter to the pot at the same time as the onion, carrot, and celery. When the butter has completely melted and the veggies are sautéing, sprinkle in the celery salt, paprika, dry mustard, salt, and flour. Stir well and cook another minute.

3. Pour beer into the mixture, stirring constantly, and cook until boiling. Stir in the chicken broth.

4. Attach lid and set regulator valve to Air Tight (closed).

5. When cooking time has elapsed, press Cancel and release the pressure manually or allow it to release naturally.

6. Remove the lid and stir. Use an immersion blender directly into the pressure pot to puree the veggies until smooth or process in a blender in batches. Turn the pressure cooker to Keep Warm.

7. Add the cheddar and cream cheese and stir until completely melted. Add the Tabasco. Finally, add the half-and-half, stir, and cook until heated through. Do not let it boil!

8. Serve hot in bowls. Offer Tabasco along with a variety of toppings and dippers.

Chicken & Sausage Gumbo

Prep Time: 30 min   **Ready in:** 40 min   **Yield:** 8–10 servings

INGREDIENTS

2 pounds chicken thighs, skin
    removed
2 teaspoons Cajun seasoning
¼ cup vegetable oil, divided
1 pound Andouille sausage, cut into
    ¼"-thick slices
3 tablespoons flour
2 medium red bell peppers, seeds and
    membrane removed, then coarsely
    chopped
1 very large yellow onion, coarsely
    chopped
2 tablespoons water
2 cloves garlic, finely minced
1 28-ounce can crushed tomato
1 28-ounce can petite diced tomatoes
2 cups chicken broth
1 tablespoon (heaping) gumbo filé
    seasoning
¼ teaspoon cayenne
2 bay leaves
⅓ cup long grain rice, uncooked
1 16-ounce bag frozen cut okra
salt and pepper to taste
Tabasco®, optional

COOK'S TIP
If you cannot find Andouille
sausage, you may substitute
smoked sausage instead.

1. Wash and pat dry the chicken thighs. Sprinkle with the Cajun seasoning. Set aside.

2. Place the pressure cooker on a level surface, insert the pressure pan, and plug in the unit.

3. Set Cook Time for 25 minutes and press Start.

4. Add 3 tablespoons of the oil to the pan. Add the sausage and cook for 5 minutes or until well browned. Remove and drain on paper towels.

5. Cook the chicken in batches to prevent overcrowding, 3 minutes per side or until brown. Drain on paper towels with the sausage until needed.

6. Add the remaining oil along with the flour to the pan and cook for 4–5 minutes or until the mixture is dark brown.

7. In the meantime, place the peppers and onion into a microwave-safe dish with 2 tablespoons of water, cover loosely with a damp paper towel, and microwave for 3 minutes. Carefully remove from microwave and stir into the browned flour until coated.

8. Add the garlic, both cans of tomatoes, chicken broth, filé, cayenne, and bay leaves. Stir well and then add the sausage and chicken back into the mixture.

(Continued on next page.)

9. Attach the lid and set the exhaust valve to Air Tight (closed).

10. While gumbo is under pressure, cook long grain rice separately, according to package directions, and set aside (you should end up with about 4 cups cooked rice).

11. When the cooking time has elapsed in the pressure cooker, unplug and let rest for 5 minutes. Place a paper towel over the vent and release the remaining pressure.

12. Carefully open the lid and stir in the okra, along with salt and pepper. Set the Cook Time for 4 minutes, reattach lid, and return valve to the closed position. Press Start.

13. When the cooking time has elapsed, let the pressure release naturally for about 10 minutes. When it is safe to open the lid, use tongs and remove the chicken to a cutting board, close the cooker lid, with the valve open, and let simmer on Keep Warm.

14. Using tongs, remove the chicken from the pot. When it is cool enough to handle, remove the meat from the bones, shred the meat, and return it to the pot. Discard bones.

15. Continue cooking on Keep Warm until the chicken is reheated throughout.

16. To serve, place about ¼ cup rice into the bottom of a bowl or cup and ladle 1 cup gumbo over the top. Taste and add Tabasco sauce if desired.

Cream of Mushroom Soup

Prep Time: 15 min   **Ready in:** 30 min   **Yield:** 8–10 servings

INGREDIENTS

4 tablespoons butter
2 shallots, finely minced
1 pound sliced mushrooms
4 cups chicken broth
1 cup water
3 tablespoons fresh tarragon leaves,
    or 1 teaspoon dried tarragon
1 tablespoon fresh thyme leaves,
    or ¼ teaspoon ground thyme
1 teaspoon salt
½ teaspoon ground black pepper
¼ cup instant mashed potato flakes
¼ cup heavy cream

COOK'S TIP

Fresh or dried, do not omit the tarragon in this dish. It adds that little flavor that keeps them guessing your recipe!

1. Place pressure cooker on a level surface, insert pressure pan, and plug in the unit.

2. Set Cook Time to 15 minutes and press Start.

3. Add butter; when melted, add shallots and mushrooms and gently sauté until tender and lightly browned. Add chicken broth, water, tarragon, thyme, salt, and pepper.

4. Attach lid and set the regulator valve to Air Tight (closed).

5. When cooking time has elapsed, press Cancel to stop the Keep Warm function. Wait 10 minutes before releasing any remaining pressure.

6. Turn the pressure cooker to Keep Warm. Stir in potato flakes. Using an immersion blender directly in the pressure pot, process the mushrooms until you reach your preferred consistency, chunky to smooth.

7. Adjust seasonings as needed and add cream. Heat until mixture is just warmed throughout. Do not boil!

Chicken Noodle Soup

Prep Time: 15 min   **Ready in:** 45–50 min   **Yield:** 8 servings

INGREDIENTS

3–4-pound whole fryer chicken
salt and pepper
2 tablespoons olive oil
1 tablespoon butter
1 medium onion, coarsely chopped
6 cups canned chicken broth
2 teaspoons kosher salt
1 teaspoon ground black pepper
1 teaspoon dried thyme
1 tablespoon dried parsley
1¼ cups chopped celery
1¼ cups chopped carrots
8 ounces wide egg noodles

1. Wash and pat dry chicken. Lightly salt and pepper chicken inside and out.

2. Place your pressure cooker on a level surface, insert the pressure pot, and plug the unit in.

3. Set Cook Time to 10 minutes or select the preprogrammed Brown button; press Start.

4. When the pan is hot, add the olive oil and butter, followed by the onion; sauté until lightly brown.

5. Add chicken broth, salt, pepper, thyme, and dried parsley. Stir well and then place chicken into pot.

6. Attach and lock the lid of your pressure cooker; set the pressure control to Air Tight (closed).

7. Press the Cancel button and reset the Cook Time for 15 minutes, or press the preprogrammed Chicken button. Press Start.

8. When cooking is complete, press Cancel to turn off the Keep Warm feature and let rest 5 minutes before manually exhausting the pressure. Once the pressure has been released, carefully open the lid and stir well.

9. Remove chicken and set aside. When cool enough to handle, remove the bones and skin from the chicken and discard. Use a slotted spoon to remove and discard any undesirable bits from the broth.

10. Cut chicken into bite-sized pieces and return to the broth. Set Cook Time to 6 minutes; press Start.

11. Allow the mixture to come to a gentle boil; add the celery, carrots, and egg noodles. Stir well. Replace pressure lid, set exhaust valve to Air Tight (closed).

12. When time has elapsed, release the pressure manually until you can remove lid.

13. Check the doneness of the noodles and serve immediately. (If more time is needed, cover and cook on Keep Warm until the noodles are tender.) Serve hot with crackers.

Tomato Basil Soup

Prep Time: 5 min   **Ready in:** 25 Min   **Yield 8–10 servings**

INGREDIENTS

1 tablespoon olive oil
1 medium onion, chopped
2 cloves garlic, finely chopped
¼ teaspoon dried thyme
½ cup fresh basil leaves, washed
    and thinly sliced (save 3–4 whole
    leaves for garnish)
2 28-ounce cans whole peeled
    tomatoes
1 cup vegetable stock
pinch of sugar
salt and pepper to taste
⅓ cup half-and-half

TV TIDBIT
Tomato soup is commonly used
in TV demos for appliances like
pressure cookers, expensive
blenders, and immersion blenders!
It's easy and delicious, but be sure
to add a small dollop of sour cream
or a swirl of cream and a basil leaf
as garnish so it looks TV ready!

1. Place pressure cooker on a level surface, insert pressure pan, and plug in the unit.

2. Set Cook Time to 10 minutes and press Start. Add oil.

3. When the oil is hot, add onion and gently sauté until tender.

4. Add garlic, thyme, and basil and sauté another minute.

5. Add the tomatoes, vegetable stock, and sugar.

6. Attach lid and set the regulator valve to Air Tight (closed).

7. When cooking time has elapsed, press Cancel to stop the Keep Warm function. Wait 5 minutes before releasing any remaining pressure.

8. Turn the pressure cooker to Keep Warm. Using an immersion blender directly in the pressure pot, process the tomatoes until smooth or to your preferred consistency.

9. Stir in the half-and-half and heat through, but do not boil!

TO MAKE CROUTONS

Preheat oven to 250°F. Melt some butter with a garlic clove in a small saucepan over low heat. Once butter is melted, remove from heat and let sit for 5 minutes. Brush both sides of 6–7 baguette slices with the butter and place on baking sheet. Bake for 10 minutes on each side.

French Onion Steak Soup

Prep Time: 10 min **Ready in:** 45 min **Yield:** 10–12 servings

INGREDIENTS
- 1 tablespoon + 2 teaspoons olive oil, divided
- salt and pepper
- ¾–1 pound prime rib, or T-Bone steak
- 2 tablespoons Worcestershire sauce, divided
- 8 cups water, divided
- 3 tablespoons beef base (Better Than Bouillon® beef base recommended)
- 4 tablespoons butter
- 2 very large Spanish or Vidalia onions (about 1½ pounds), quartered and sliced ¼" thick
- 2 tablespoons flour
- provolone cheese (1 round slice for each serving)
- Parmesan cheese, finely shredded
- garlic croutons (store bought or homemade as directed)

1. Place the pressure cooker on a level surface, insert the pressure pan, and plug in the unit. Set Cook Time to 15 minutes or choose the preprogrammed Meat button; press Start.

2. Add 2 teaspoons olive oil. Lightly salt and pepper both sides of the steak, and when oil is hot, place steak into the pan and sear on both sides. Sprinkle 1 tablespoon Worcestershire sauce over the steak and ½ cup water around the steak.

3. Attach lid and set the regulator valve to Air Tight (closed). When cooking time has elapsed, release the pressure manually and carefully open the lid. Transfer steak onto a plate; when cool enough to handle, trim all fat and cut steak into small bite-sized pieces. Set aside.

4. Set Cook Time to 10 minutes and press Start. When liquid in pot begins to boil, stir in the remaining tablespoon of Worcestershire sauce, the beef base, and remaining 7½ cups water. Bring liquid to a boil and cook 3–4 minutes, stirring often. Press Cancel and carefully pour the liquid into a bowl or large measuring cup and set aside.

5. Wash, dry, and replace the pressure pot into the cooker. Set Cook Time to 10 minutes; press Start. Add butter and 1 tablespoon olive oil into the pan; when hot, add sliced onions. Cook 2–3 minutes, stirring constantly until onions begin to brown. Add the steak to the onions. Sprinkle flour over the meat and onions; gently toss and cook until heated through. Slowly pour in the reserved broth and stir well.

6. Attach lid and set the regulator valve to Air Tight (closed). When cooking time has elapsed, manually release the pressure and carefully open the lid.

7. To assemble: Place 1 large crouton (or 3–4 small croutons) into the bottom of each oven-proof soup crock. Ladle soup over croutons. Top with a slice of provolone and a generous sprinkling of the shredded Parmesan cheese. Place under the broiler until cheese begins to melt and brown.

Beef, Barley & Vegetable Soup

Prep Time: 10 min   **Ready in:** 1 hour   **Yield:** 8–10 servings

INGREDIENTS

2 tablespoons vegetable oil
1 medium onion, diced
2 stalks celery, sliced
1 clove garlic, minced
6 cups water, divided
3 tablespoons beef base (Better Than Bouillon® beef base recommended), or 6 beef bouillon cubes
2 pounds beef cubes for stew
2 medium bay leaves
½ cup medium barley (uncooked)
1 14½-ounce can petite diced tomatoes
1 9-ounce package frozen mixed vegetables

COOK'S TIP
Additional water may be needed if soup becomes too thick upon standing.

1. Place the pressure cooker on a level surface, insert the pressure pan, and plug in the unit.

2. Set Cook Time to 20 minutes and press Start.

3. Add the oil to the cooker. When the oil is hot, add the onion, celery, and garlic and sauté for 3–4 minutes.

4. Add 1 cup of water and all of the beef base or bouillon cubes; stir until bouillon is dissolved.

5. Add the beef, the remaining 5 cups water, and bay leaves.

6. Attach lid and set the regulator valve to Air Tight (closed).

7. When cooking time has elapsed, press Cancel to stop the Keep Warm function. Wait 5 minutes before releasing any remaining pressure.

8. Add the barley and diced tomatoes. Reattach lid, set valve to Air Tight (closed). Set Cook Time for 20 minutes and press Start.

9. When cooking time has elapsed, press Cancel to stop the Keep Warm function. Wait 5 minutes before releasing any remaining pressure.

10. Carefully open the lid and stir in the frozen vegetables.

11. Reattach lid and set valve to Air Tight (closed). Set Cook Time for 2 minutes and press Start.

12. When cook time is up, unplug machine and let pressure release naturally.

Potato Leek Soup

Prep Time: 15 min   **Ready in:** 30 min   **Yield:** 8–10 servings

INGREDIENTS

1 large leek, green tops removed
4 tablespoons butter
4 cups chicken broth
1 cup water
8 medium white potatoes, peeled and
    quartered
1 teaspoon salt
½ teaspoon ground black pepper +
    extra for serving
½ cup heavy cream

1. Thinly slice only the whites of the leek (you should end up with about 1–1¼ cups).

2. Place pressure cooker on a level surface, insert pressure pan, and plug in the unit.

3. Set Cook Time to 15 minutes and press Start.

4. Add butter to pan; when butter is melted, add leeks and gently sauté until tender but not browned. Add chicken broth, water, potatoes, salt, and pepper.

5. Attach lid and set the regulator valve to Air Tight (closed).

6. When cooking time has elapsed, press Cancel to stop the Keep Warm function. Wait 10 minutes before releasing any remaining pressure.

7. Turn the pressure cooker to Keep Warm. Using an immersion blender directly in the pressure pot, blend potatoes and leeks until completely smooth.

8. Adjust seasonings as needed and add cream. Heat until mixture is just warmed throughout. Do not boil!

9. Serve hot with freshly ground black pepper.

Tuscan Bean Soup

Prep Time: 10 min   **Ready in:** 45 min   **Yield:** 10–12 servings

INGREDIENTS

6 Italian sausages
  (about 1¼–1½ pounds)
1 cup water
2 tablespoons olive oil
1 4-ounce piece of salt pork
1 medium onion, chopped
2 celery ribs, thickly sliced
1 carrot, thinly sliced
2 cloves garlic, chopped
4 cups chicken stock or broth
1 28-ounce can Italian peeled
  tomatoes, drained and chopped
1 head escarole or collard greens,
  leaves cut into 3-inch pieces
3 19-ounce cans cannellini beans
  (white kidney beans)
2 15½-ounce cans dark red kidney
  beans
salt and pepper
crushed red pepper flakes, *optional*
grated Romano cheese, *optional*

COOK'S TIP
To use dried beans, consult the time
chart (see page 179) and precook
the beans before going on to step 2.

1. Place the pressure cooker on a level surface, insert the pressure pan, and plug in the unit.

2. Prick sausages all over with a fork. Place into the pressure pan along with water.

3. Attach lid and set the regulator valve to Air Tight (closed). Set Cook Time to 10 minutes and press Start.

4. When cooking time has elapsed, release the pressure manually and carefully open the lid. Transfer the sausages to a plate and drain the liquid from the pot.

5. Place the pot back into the cooker, set Cook Time to 10 minutes, and press Start.

6. Add the oil to the cooker. When the oil is hot, add the salt pork, onion, celery, carrot, and garlic and sauté for 3–4 minutes. Add the chicken stock, tomatoes, greens, and both types of beans. Stir well.

7. Chop the Italian Sausages into bite-sized pieces and add to mixture.

8. Attach lid and set the regulator valve to Air Tight (closed).

9. When cooking time has elapsed, press Cancel to stop the Keep Warm function. Let pressure release naturally.

10. Remove and discard the salt pork. Stir well, taste, and adjust with salt and pepper as needed.

11. Serve in bowls, offering crushed red pepper flakes and grated Romano cheese on the side.

Fresh Vegetables

Fresh Vegetables

Tips for Cooking Vegetables

- Vegetables cooked in the pressure cooker are second only to raw when it comes to nutrients! The airtight environment will reinfuse the vital nutrients back into the foods along with any seasonings added. Be careful not to overseason.
- Cut vegetables into uniform-sized pieces to ensure even cooking. If cooking a variety of vegetables, cut them into pieces large to small in order of their cooking times. For example, cut pieces of squash and zucchini into 1" pieces and carrots into ¼" pieces if cooking for the same length of time.
- Use a steam basket whenever possible to keep the vegetables above the water; this will prevent burning and help retain vital nutrients.
- Use the minimum amount of water or stock as directed by your pressure cooker's manual.
- If cooking frozen vegetables, use the same amount of water as directed on the package, but cook for the same amount of time as you would fresh vegetables.
- As in all pressure cooking, the cook time starts WHEN PRESSURE IS REACHED. Set your timer correctly to avoid overcooking! You can always add more time if necessary, so when in doubt, choose the quickest time.
- Use the Quick Release Method for releasing the steam to avoid overcooking the vegetables.
- Refer to the following time chart and have fun experimenting with different liquids. Try broth, wine, and fruit juices for bold new flavors!

Vegetable Cooking Times

All cook times are based on a 12 PSI electric pressure cooker. To adjust, see Adapting Your Favorite Recipes on pages 2–3.

Vegetable	Max Quantity	Minimum Liquid	Minimum Cook Time (minutes)	Release Method
Artichoke, large whole	6–8	1 cup	13–14	quick or natural
Artichoke, medium whole	8–10	1 cup	11–12	quick or natural
Artichoke, small whole	half-full	1 cup	9–10	quick or natural
Artichoke, hearts	3 cups	1 cup	5–6	quick
Asparagus, fine, whole	1–2 lbs.	¾ cup	3–4	quick
Asparagus, thick, whole	1–2 lbs.	¾ cup	5–6	quick
Beans, green, whole (fresh or frozen)	1–2 lbs.	¾ cup	4–5	quick
Beets, ¼" slices	2 cups	¾ cup	8	quick or natural
Beets, medium whole, peeled	half-full	¾ cup	13–14	quick or natural
Beets, large whole, peeled	half-full	1 cup	20–22	quick or natural
Broccoli, florets or spears	half-full	¾ cups	3	quick
Brussels sprouts, whole	1–2 lbs.	¾ cup	8–9	quick
Cabbage, red or green, quartered	half-full	1 cup	5	quick
Carrots, ¼" slices	2 cups	¾ cup	3–4	quick
Carrots, 1" chunks, or whole baby	2 cups	¾ cup	5–6	quick
Cauliflower, florets	half-full	¾ cup	5–6	quick
Cauliflower, whole head	1–2 lbs.	¾ cup	7–8	quick
Collard greens	¾ full	1 cup	6	quick
Corn on the cob	6–8	¾ cup	7–8	quick or natural
Eggplant, 1" chunks or slices	2 cups	¾ cup	4	quick
Endive or escarole, coarsely chopped	¾ full	1 cup	4	quick
Kale	¾ full	1 cup	4	quick
Leeks, white parts cut in 1" rings	half-full	¾ cup	4	quick
Mixed vegetables, frozen	3 cups	¾ cup	3	quick

Vegetable	Max Quantity	Minimum Liquid	Minimum Cook Time (minutes)	Release Method
Okra, whole medium	3 cups	¾ cup	4	quick
Onions, baby pearl	3 cups	¾ cup	3	quick
Onions, whole medium peeled	half-full	1 cup	5	quick
Parsnips, 1" cubes or slices	3 cups	1 cup	5	quick
Peas, in pod (e.g., snow peas)	3 cups	¾ cup	2	quick
Peas, fresh green	NOT RECOMMENDED			quick
Peas, fresh black eyes, conch, purple hull, etc.	half-full	¾ cup	7–8	natural
Potatoes, small or new, whole	half-full	¾ cup	6–7	quick or natural
Potatoes, 1" cubes or slices	half-full	¾ cup	6–7	quick or natural
Potatoes, whole medium	¾ full	¾ cup	10–11	quick or natural
Potatoes, whole large	¾ full	1 cup	14–15	quick or natural
Pumpkin, 2" chunks or slices	3 cups	¾ cup	4–5	quick
Rutabaga, 1" chunks	2 cups	¾ cup	6–7	quick
Spinach, fresh	¾ full	¾ cup	2	quick
Spinach, frozen	¾ full	¾ cup	2	quick
Squash, acorn, halved	2	1 cup	10–11	quick
Squash, butternut, 1" cubes or slices	half-full	¾ cup	5–6	quick
Squash, yellow crook neck, 1" rings	half-full	¾ cup	3	quick
Squash, yellow crook neck, whole medium	¾ full	¾ cup	5–6	quick
Sweet potato, peeled, 1½" slices	3 cups	¾ cup	7–8	quick or natural
Sweet potato, peeled, whole medium or halved large	half-full	¾ cup	12–13	quick or natural
Swiss chard	¾ full	¾ cup	2	quick
Tomatoes, plum or Roma, whole medium	¾ full	¾ cup	2–3	natural
Turnip, small–medium, quartered and greens	3 cups	¾ cup	7–8	quick
Zucchini, ½" slices or chunks	3 cups	¾ cup	2–3	quick

Perfect Green Beans

Prep Time: 5 min   **Ready in:** 9 min   **Yield:** 4–6 servings

INGREDIENTS

1 small white or yellow onion, peeled
¾ cup hot water
1 tablespoon beef base (Better than Bouillon® beef base recommended)
2 tablespoons butter
½ teaspoon ground black pepper
1–2 pounds fresh whole green beans, ends trimmed
salt and fresh ground pepper, for serving

COOK'S TIP
Try adding a clove of garlic or diced cooked bacon to give everyday green beans a flavor boost!

1. Place your pressure cooker on a level surface, insert the pressure pot, and plug the unit in.

2. Prepare the onion by peeling it and then cutting it in half so that one side is the bottom half with the roots, and the other is the upper half. On the half with the roots, score an X shape into the flat face with a knife. Set aside. (You don't need the upper half; save it for another recipe.)

3. In a glass measuring cup or small bowl, mix the hot water and beef base until dissolved.

4. On pressure cooker, set Cook Time to 4 minutes (or use Vegetable setting and decrease time) and press the Start button. Add the butter; when it begins to melt, place the onion face down into the butter. Cook quickly for 1–2 minutes, but do not let the butter brown. Add the water/bouillon along with the pepper.

5. Toss in the green beans.

6. Attach and lock the lid of your pressure cooker.

7. Set the pressure control to Air Tight (closed).

8. When cooking time has elapsed, release the pressure manually by opening the pressure control valve to exhaust.

9. Once the pressure has been released, carefully open the lid, discard the onion, and serve immediately with salt and fresh ground pepper.

Brussels Sprouts

Prep Time: 5 min   **Ready in:** 16 min   **Yield:** 4–6 servings

INGREDIENTS

1 teaspoon olive oil
1 cup red onion, coarsely chopped
1¼ pounds fresh Brussels sprouts,
   ends trimmed, brown leaves
   removed
1 tablespoon balsamic vinegar
   (good quality)
¾ cup chicken broth
½ teaspoon salt
½ teaspoon freshly ground black
   pepper
Parmesan cheese, grated or shaved
   (optional)

COOK'S TIP

For the chicken broth in
this recipe, I use 1 teaspoon
Better Than Bouillon®
chicken base dissolved in
¾ cup of water.

1. Place your pressure cooker on a level surface, insert the pressure pot, and plug the unit in.

2. Select the Browning feature of your pressure cooker, or set Cook Time to 10 minutes, and press the Start button.

3. Add olive oil to the pot; when oil is hot, add onions.

4. Sauté, stirring often, for 1–2 minutes until onion begins to soften but do not turn brown.

5. Add Brussels sprouts, balsamic vinegar, chicken broth, salt, and pepper to the pot; stir, close, and lock the lid of your pressure cooker.

6. Set the pressure control to Air Tight (closed).

7. Press Cancel to stop the browning function; set new cook time for 9 minutes and press Start.

8. When cooking time has elapsed, release the pressure manually by opening the pressure control valve to exhaust.

9. Once the pressure has been released, carefully open the lid and transfer Brussels sprouts to a serving dish. Sprinkle with Parmesan cheese if desired. Serve immediately.

Parsley Potatoes

Prep Time: 1 min **Ready in:** 15 min **Yield:** 4–6 servings

INGREDIENTS

8 tablespoons butter, divided
3 cloves garlic, peeled whole
2 teaspoons salt
10–15 fingerling potatoes (assorted colors), or red new potatoes, washed
cool water (enough to cover potatoes)
¼ cup chopped parsley

1. Place your pressure cooker on a level surface, insert the pressure pot, and plug the unit in.

2. Add 4 tablespoons butter, garlic, and salt.

3. When butter is almost melted, add the potatoes. Add just enough water to cover the potatoes.

4. Attach and lock the lid of your pressure cooker; set the pressure control to Air Tight (closed).

5. Set Cook Time to 10 minutes and press the Start button.

6. When cooking time has elapsed, release the pressure manually by opening the pressure control valve to exhaust.

7. Once the pressure has been released, carefully open the lid.

8. Drain the potatoes. Place cooked potatoes back into the pressure pan along with the remaining 4 tablespoons butter and the chopped parsley. Leave on Keep Warm for up to 15 minutes before gently tossing and serving.

Buttery Corn-on-the-Cob

Prep Time: 5–10 min 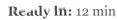   **Ready In:** 12 min   **Yield:** 4–6 servings

INGREDIENTS

4–12 ears of fresh corn, husk and silk removed
8 tablespoons butter
⅓ cup water
2 teaspoons salt
¼ teaspoon granulated sugar

TV TIDBIT

When cooking corn-on-the-cob on TV, we often stack the corn on end so that we can show a larger capacity. If you want to cook the corn this way, I suggest you use 2 cups of water, brought to an almost-boil, before adding the corn to the pot. This will prevent the corn from burning on the bottom.

1. Place your pressure cooker on a level surface, insert the pressure pot, and plug the unit in.

2. If you have a low rack or trivet for your pressure cooker, place it inside the pot. Add all ingredients.

3. Attach and lock the lid of your pressure cooker; set the pressure control to Air Tight (closed).

4. Set Cook Time to 7 minutes and press the Start button.

5. When cooking time has elapsed, manually release the pressure by opening the pressure control valve to exhaust.

6. Once the pressure has been released, open the lid carefully and stir.

7. Use tongs to transfer corn to a platter, ladle butter sauce over corn, and serve immediately.

Agave Carrots

Prep Time: 5 min   **Ready in:** 12 min   **Yield:** 4–6 servings

INGREDIENTS
1 pound baby carrots
1 tablespoon butter
½ cup water
2 teaspoons agave light syrup
1 teaspoon orange zest
2 teaspoons fresh parsley (optional)

1. Place your pressure cooker on a level surface, insert the pressure pot, and plug the unit in.

2. Add all ingredients except for the parsley; stir.

3. Attach and lock the lid of your pressure cooker; set the pressure control to Air Tight (closed).

4. Set Cook Time to 7 minutes and press the Start button.

5. When cooking time has elapsed, release the pressure manually by opening the pressure control valve to exhaust.

6. Once the pressure has been released, carefully open the lid and stir. Transfer carrots to a serving dish.

7. Sprinkle the fresh parsley over the carrots, if desired, and serve immediately.

Artichokes

Prep Time: 10 min   **Ready in:** 18 min   **Yield:** 4 servings, or 12–15 appetizer servings

INGREDIENTS

4 large artichokes, stems trimmed and leaf tips snipped
1 stick of butter, cut into pieces (½ cup)
2 cloves garlic, peeled and thinly sliced
¼ cup water
¼ cup dry white wine
1 lemon, zested, then halved and juiced

For the dip:
¼ cup mayonnaise
1 teaspoon lemon juice
¼ teaspoon garlic salt

TV TIDBIT
Whenever we cook artichokes on the Home Shopping Network, everyone scrambles after the show to grab a doggie bag! I always try to get at least two, and since this demo is done in a 10-quart pressure cooker, there are *plenty* to go around!

1. Trim the bottom of the artichokes so that they will stand up.

2. Tuck pieces of butter and slices of garlic randomly throughout the leaves of the artichokes.

3. Place your pressure cooker on a level surface, insert the pressure pot, and plug the unit in.

4. Place the artichokes into the bottom of the pressure cooker (or into a steamer basket). Mix the liquids together with the lemon zest and pour over all.

5. Attach and lock the lid of your pressure cooker; set the pressure control to Air Tight (closed).

6. Set Cook Time to 15 minutes and press the Start button.

7. When cooking time has elapsed, release the pressure manually by opening the pressure control valve to exhaust.

8. Once the pressure has been released, open the lid carefully.

9. Use tongs to transfer artichokes to individual dishes or to one large platter. Ladle the sauce from the pan over top.

10. Serve hot with a cold dip made from mayonnaise, lemon juice, and garlic salt.

Red Cabbage Kraut

Prep Time: 15 min **Ready in:** 20 min **Yield:** 10–12 servings

INGREDIENTS
6 slices bacon, coarsely chopped
1 large onion, finely chopped
1 very large red cabbage, shredded
1 tablespoon + 2 teaspoons salt
1 tablespoon ground black pepper
2 bay leaves
½ cup white vinegar
1 apple, cored and chopped
½ cup water

1. Place your pressure cooker on a level surface, insert the pressure pot, and plug the unit in.

2. Set Cook Time to 10 minutes and press Start.

3. When the pan is hot, add the bacon; stir quickly and cook until beginning to brown.

4. Add the onion and cook another 3–4 minutes or until the onion begins to soften but is not browned.

5. Add the remaining ingredients and stir gently to mix.

6. Attach and lock the lid of your pressure cooker; set the pressure control to Air Tight (closed).

7. Press the Cancel button and reset the cook time for 10 minutes; press Start.

8. When cooking is complete, cancel the Keep Warm feature and let rest 5 minutes before exhausting the pressure manually.

9. Once the pressure has been released, open the lid carefully and stir well. Serve.

Swiss Chard
with Warm Bacon Vinaigrette

Prep Time: 15 min **Ready in:** 20 min **Yield:** 6–8 servings

INGREDIENTS

4 slices bacon

1 medium red onion, cut in strips

¾ cup water

1 tablespoon + 2 teaspoons salt

1 tablespoon ground black pepper

1¼ pounds Swiss chard, chopped (about 20 ounces, or 24 cups)

1 tablespoon cider vinegar

1. Place your pressure cooker on a level surface, insert the pressure pot, and plug the unit in.

2. Set Cook Time to 3 minutes and press Start.

3. When the pan is hot, add the bacon; stir quickly and cook until crispy; remove to drain on paper towel and set aside.

4. Add the onion to the bacon grease and cook another 3–4 minutes or until the onion begins to soften. While the onion is cooking, chop the bacon and set aside again.

5. Add the water to the pressure cooker and scrape the bottom of the pan. Add the salt and pepper. Add the Swiss chard to the top of the water; do not stir.

6. Attach and lock the lid of your pressure cooker; set the pressure control to Air Tight (closed).

7. When cooking is complete, cancel the Keep Warm feature and let rest 5 minutes before exhausting the pressure manually.

8. Once the pressure has been released, carefully open the lid and stir well. Stir in the vinegar.

9. Drain before serving and top with the chopped bacon.

Cauliflower

Prep Time: 15 min   **Ready in:** 25 min   **Yield:** 6–8 servings

INGREDIENTS
1 head cauliflower
¾ cup water
1 tablespoon salt
2–3 tablespoons butter, sliced in pats
½ cup shredded cheese
salt and pepper, for serving

1. Prepare the cauliflower by trimming off any green leaves, excessive stem, and brown spots.

2. Place your pressure cooker on a level surface, insert the pressure pot, and plug the unit in.

3. Set Cook Time to 8 minutes and press Start.

4. Add water to the bottom of the pot along with salt.

5. Place a rack into the cooker and set the cauliflower on the rack.

6. Attach and lock the lid of your pressure cooker; set the pressure control to Air Tight (closed).

7. When cooking is complete, cancel the Keep Warm feature and immediately exhaust the pressure.

8. Once the pressure has been released, open the lid carefully.

9. Lay the pats of butter on the cauliflower along with the shredded cheese. Replace lid, keeping the pressure valve in the Exhaust position.

10. Wait 2–3 minutes, or until the cheese is melting, and transfer the cauliflower to a serving dish. Serve hot with salt and pepper.

Cheesy Garlic Smashed Potatoes

Prep Time: 1 min   **Ready in:** 12 min   **Yield:** 4–6 servings

INGREDIENTS

10 medium white potatoes, halved
   and peeled
3 cloves garlic, peeled whole
3 teaspoons salt, divided
cool water, to cover potatoes
1 teaspoon coarsely ground black
   pepper
4 tablespoons butter, melted
¾ cup half-and-half, warmed (plus
   extra if desired)
1 cup shredded sharp cheddar

COOK'S TIP
To make "dirty" smashed potatoes, peel only 7 of the potatoes and leave the skins on 3 of them.

COOK'S TIP
Make this into a great take-along side dish! Simply spread the smashed potatoes into a buttered casserole dish, top with extra cheese, and bake for 10 minutes in a 375°F oven!

1. Place your pressure cooker on a level surface, insert the pressure pot, and plug the unit in.

2. Add halved potatoes, garlic, and 2 teaspoons salt.

3. Add just enough water to cover the potatoes.

4. Attach and lock the lid of your pressure cooker; set the pressure control to Air Tight (closed).

5. Set Cook Time to 10 minutes and press the Start button.

6. When cooking time has elapsed, release the pressure manually by opening the pressure control valve to exhaust.

7. Once the pressure has been released, open the lid carefully.

8. Drain the potatoes. Place cooked potatoes into a medium mixing bowl and add the remaining salt, pepper, butter, and half-and-half.

9. Using the medium speed of your hand mixer, whip to desired consistency, adding more half-and-half if needed. Add cheese and mix on lowest speed.

10. Adjust salt and pepper to taste and serve immediately.

Sweet Potato Mash

Prep Time: 5 min **Ready in:** 30 min **Yield:** 4–6 se

INGREDIENTS
3–4 large sweet potatoes, peeled and halved
4 tablespoons butter, divided
4 cups water
1 cup orange juice
3 teaspoons salt
¼ teaspoon cinnamon
⅛ teaspoon nutmeg
¼ cup warm milk (optional)
butter, for serving
toasted pecans, chopped, for serving

COOK'S TIP
Make this into a great holiday take-along side dish! Simply spread potatoes into a buttered casserole dish, top with pecans or marshmallows, and bake for 10 minutes in a 375°F oven!

1. Place your pressure cooker on a ` surface, insert the pressure pot, and plug the unit in.

2. Add halved potatoes and 2 tablespoons of the butter.

3. Add water and orange juice. This should almost cover the potatoes; add more water if needed.

4. Attach and lock the lid of your pressure cooker; set the pressure control to Air Tight (closed).

5. Press the preprogrammed Yams/Potato button, or Set Cook Time to 13 minutes; press Start.

6. When cooking time has elapsed, release the pressure manually and open the lid carefully.

7. Drain the potatoes, saving 1 cup of the liquid. Place cooked potatoes into a medium mixing bowl and add the remaining 2 tablespoons butter along with the salt, cinnamon, and nutmeg.

8. Using the medium speed of your hand mixer, whip to desired consistency, slowly adding the hot liquid from the potatoes. If creamier texture is desired, add the milk as well.

9. Serve immediately with butter and toasted pecans, if desired.

Asparagus

Prep Time: 15 min   **Ready in:** 15 min   **Yield:** 6–8 servings

INGREDIENTS

1 pound asparagus, thin to medium stalks
2 tablespoons butter
2 cloves garlic, minced
1 teaspoon salt
1 tablespoon ground black pepper
¾ cup water

1. Prepare the asparagus by trimming off the woody end where they naturally break when bending the stalk.

2. Place your pressure cooker on a level surface, insert the pressure pot, and plug the unit in.

3. Set Cook Time to 3 minutes and press Start.

4. Add butter to the pot, along with the garlic, salt, and pepper.

5. Place the asparagus directly in the pan and toss in the butter. Pour the water over the asparagus.

6. Attach and lock the lid of your pressure cooker; set the pressure control to Air Tight (closed).

7. When cooking is complete, cancel the Keep Warm feature and immediately exhaust the pressure.

8. Once the pressure has been released, open the lid carefully. Use tongs to remove. Serve immediately.

Cranberry Stuffing

Prep Time: 10 min   **Ready in:** 30 min   **Yield:** 4–6 servings

INGREDIENTS

4 tablespoons butter
½ cup onion, minced
½ cup celery, minced
¼ cup fresh parsley, chopped
1½ cups chicken broth
12-ounce package Pepperidge Farm®
    cubed herb-seasoned stuffing
¼–¾ cup whole cranberries

1. Place your pressure cooker on a level surface, insert the pressure pot, and plug the unit in. Select the Brown or Sauté setting, or set the Cook Time to 5 minutes.

2. Add the butter, onion, celery, parsley, and chicken broth.

3. When the liquid begins to boil, add the stuffing cubes and cranberries. Quickly toss to moisten.

4. Immediately attach and lock the lid of your pressure cooker; set the pressure control to Air Tight (closed). Press Cancel to stop the browning function.

5. Press the preprogrammed Seafood button, or set cook time to 3 minutes; press Start.

6. When cooking time has elapsed, immediately release the pressure. Open the lid carefully.

7. Use as stuffing for a turkey or chicken, serve immediately as is, or spoon into a baking dish and brown in the oven.

COOK'S TIP

Get an oven-baked style of stuffing by placing the stuffing in a buttered casserole dish and baking for 10 minutes in a 400°F oven!

COOK'S TIP

The cranberries tend to make this stuffing a bit tart, so do not use more than ¾ cup. You may even want to reduce to ¼ cup cranberries your first time and adjust from there.

Beef, Pork & Lamb

Beef, Pork & Lamb

SLOW COOK FAST!

If you use your pressure cooker for only one thing—use it for large cuts of meat!

Ribs and roasts cook deliciously in a fraction of the time and yield that fall-off-the-bone tenderness meat lovers crave!

Meat Cooking Times

Meat	Brown?	Minimum Liquid	Minimum Cook Time (minutes)	Release Method
Red Meat				
Beef brisket, fresh or corned (3–4 lbs.)	no	2 cups	50–75	natural
Beef cubes or stew meat, 1–1½" (up to 3 lbs.)	yes	1 cup	15–20	natural
Beef heart (3–4 lbs.)	no	cover	50–75	natural
Beef kidney	no	cover	8–10	natural
Beef liver, sliced	yes	1 cup	5	natural
Beef meatballs (1–2 lbs.)	yes	1 cup	10–12	natural
Beef meatloaf (2–3 lbs.)	no	1 cup	15–20	natural
Beef oxtails	yes	cover	40–45	natural
Beef pot roast, rib, round, rump, chuck, or blade (3–4 lbs.)	yes	2 cups	50–60	natural
Beef shank (1½–2½" thick)	yes	1½ cups	35–45	natural
Beef short ribs (3–4 lbs.)	yes	1½ cups	30–40	natural
Beef steak, rump, round, chuck, or blade, 1–2" thick (up to 3 lbs.)	yes	1 cup	20–25	natural
Beef tongue, fresh or smoked (2–3 lbs.)	no	cover	75–90	natural
Beef tripe honeycomb (2 lbs.)	no	cover	40–45	natural
Goat, young			Cook as for similar cuts of lamb	
Goat, mature			Cook as for similar cuts of venison	

(Continued on next page.)

Meat	Brown?	Minimum Liquid	Minimum Cook Time (minutes)	Release Method
Lamb chops, ½" thick	yes	¾ cup	5	quick
Lamb chops, 1" thick	yes	¾ cup	9	quick
Lamb leg (3 lbs.)	yes	1½ cups	20–25	natural
Lamb shoulder roast, bone-in (3–5 lbs.)	yes	2 cups	25–35	natural
Lamb stew meat, 1" cubes	yes	1 cup	12–15	natural
Veal chops, up to 1" thick	yes	¾ cup	5–7	quick
Veal shanks, up to 3" thick	yes	1 cup	25–35	natural
Veal stew meat, 1" cubes (up to 2 lbs.)	yes	2 cups	10–12	natural
Venison roast, any cut, 3–4" thick	yes	2 cups	40–45	natural
Venison, cubed, thin-sliced, steaks, or chops, up to 1" thick	yes	¾ cup	20–25	natural
Venison, ground meat	yes	¾ cup	12–15	natural

Meat	Brown?	Minimum Liquid	Minimum Cook Time (minutes)	Release Method
Pork				
Pork, ham hocks, smoked	no	cover	45	natural
Pork, ham picnic or shoulder (fresh, uncooked, 3–5 lbs.)	no	2½ cups	40–50	natural
Pork, ham shank or butt (fresh, uncooked, 3–5 lbs.)	no	2½ cups	50–60	natural
Pork chops or steaks, up to 1" thick	yes	¾ cup	6	natural
Pork chops or steaks, over 1" thick or stuffed	yes	¾ cup	8–10	natural
Pork loin roast (3–4 lbs.)	yes	1 cup	25–35	natural
Pork, pigs feet	no	cover	45	natural
Pork ribs, spareribs, baby back, bone-in, single rack (grillable, up to 4 lbs.)	no	¾ cup	40	natural
Pork ribs, spareribs, baby back, bone-in, single rack (fall-off-the-bone, up to 4 lbs.)	no	1 cup	55	natural
Pork shoulder, arm, or blade roast, bone-in or boneless shreddable, 3–4 lbs.)	yes	2 cups	45–50	natural
Pork sausage, Italian, Polish, kielbasa (steam on rack)	yes	¾ cup	8	quick
Pork stew meat, 1½" cubes	yes	¾ cup	10–12	natural

Meatloaf Minis

Prep Time: 15 min **Ready in:** 1 hour 🍴 **Yield:** each loaf serves 2

INGREDIENTS

1 large egg, beaten
5 tablespoons tomato paste, divided
1 small onion, minced (about ¼ cup)
¼ small red or green bell pepper,
    minced (about ½ cup)
1 clove garlic, minced
2 teaspoons dried parsley, or
    2 tablespoons fresh chopped
    parsley
1 teaspoon dried thyme, or 1
    tablespoon fresh chopped thyme
½ cup seasoned bread crumbs
2¼ pounds extra lean ground beef
1 cup shredded mozzarella cheese,
    divided
¾ cup water

1. Prepare the meatloaves by beating the egg in the bottom of a large mixing bowl. Add in 2 tablespoons of the tomato paste, followed by the onion, bell pepper, garlic, parsley, thyme, and bread crumbs. Mix in the ground beef, followed by ½ cup of the mozzarella cheese. Use your hands to blend as evenly as possible.

2. Divide the meat in half and make 2 loaves.

3. Place pressure cooker on a level surface, insert the pot, and plug in the unit. Set Cook Time to 25 minutes; press Start.

4. Whisk 1 tablespoon of tomato paste into the water; pour into the pressure cooker.

5. Place the meatloaves into the pot.

6. Secure the lid and turn pressure valve to Air Tight (closed).

7. When the cooking time has elapsed, turn the Keep Warm feature off and let pressure release naturally.

8. While the pressure is releasing, preheat the broiler in your oven on the low setting.

9. When the pressure has released, open the lid carefully.

10. Use tongs and a spatula to move meat loaves carefully from the pot to a cookie sheet. Spread the top of the meatloaves with the remaining 2 tablespoons of tomato paste and sprinkle with the remaining ½ cup of shredded mozzarella.

11. Place the cookie sheet with the meatloaves into the oven on a low-center rack. Broil until tomato and cheese are hot and bubbly. Serve with mashed or scalloped potatoes.

Corned Beef

Prep Time: 15 min   **Ready in:** 1 hour 10 min   **Yield:** 1 serving per ⅓ pound meat

INGREDIENTS

3–7-pound corned beef with
   seasoning packet
1 teaspoon onion salt
1 teaspoon celery salt
1 tablespoon brown sugar
1 tablespoon coarse ground mustard
1 bottle of beer (Darker is better, but
   it's up to you!)
cool water
6–15 small red potatoes, peeled if
   desired
½ pound baby carrots, or 1"-round
   slices of large carrots
1 small–medium head cabbage,
   cut in half lengthwise, hard core
   removed, chopped into large bite-
   sized pieces (do not shred or finely
   chop!)
stone ground mustard, or prepared
   horseradish, for serving

COOK'S TIP

To keep your veggies fresh before cooking, place all the veggies into a large bowl, cover with a wet paper towel, and place in the fridge until ready to use.

1. Prepare the meat by removing the corned beef from the package and rinsing off the surface brine. Lay the corned beef on a cutting board and sprinkle the onion salt, celery salt, brown sugar, and mustard over the meat. Use your hands to massage the seasonings into the meat.

2. Looking at the pot of your pressure cooker, decide if the meat must be cut down to fit inside. Ideally, you will leave the meat whole and either stand it on end, "curling" it along the inside edge (fat side out), or just lay it inside the pot flat or arched (fat side up). However, if it is just too large, cut the meat in half or however is necessary to fit!

3. When the meat is in the pot, sprinkle in the seasoning packet and add the bottle of beer. Fill the pot with cool water until the meat is submerged by 1 inch.

4. Plug in the pressure cooker, secure the lid, and set pressure valve to Air Tight (closed).

5. Set Cook Time for 1 hour and 15 minutes. Press Start.

6. When cooking time has elapsed, turn the pressure cooker off. Let sit 10 minutes and then release the remaining pressure. Open the lid carefully and remove the meat to a cutting board. Let the liquid remain untouched in the pot.

7. When cool enough to handle, use a sharp knife to slice away the majority of the fat on the meat; discard.

8. Using a measuring cup or turkey baster, carefully remove as much fatty oil as you can from the top of the liquid in the pot. You want to leave a small amount of fat to season the vegetables, so do not use a separator.

9. Reload the pot first with the potatoes and carrots, then with the meat, and top with the cabbage. The liquid should not fill the pot. You should have 4 inches of liquid-less space at the top of the pot. If you find that you now have too much liquid, use a measuring cup or baster to remove excess.

10. Replace the lid, set the valve to Air Tight (closed), and set the Cook Time to 15 minutes; press Start.

11. When the time has elapsed, turn the pressure cooker off and let the pressure release naturally.

12. Open the lid carefully and remove the meat to a cutting board.

13. To serve, slice the meat against the grain and serve with the vegetables and a generous dollop of stone ground mustard or prepared horseradish.

Sunday Roast

Prep Time: 15 min   **Ready in:** 1 hour 10 min **Yield:** 1 serving per ⅓ pound meat

INGREDIENTS

2 tablespoons vegetable oil
3–4-pound round roast
1 tablespoon balsamic vinegar
½ cup red wine (good quality)
1 medium onion, coarsely chopped
1 clove garlic, minced
1 tablespoon Worcestershire sauce
1 tablespoon ketchup
1 tablespoon beef bouillon base
    (Better Than Bouillon® beef base
    recommended)
1 teaspoon salt
1 teaspoon coarse ground black
    pepper
1 teaspoon chopped fresh rosemary
    (plus extra for garnish)
1½ cups hot water
8–10 small fingerling potatoes
8–10 baby carrots

For the gravy:
3 tablespoons butter
2 tablespoons flour
3 cups strained stock, from making
    the roast
3 tablespoons cream, or whole milk

1. Place your pressure cooker on a level surface, insert the pressure pot, and plug the unit in.

2. Set Cook Time for 10 minutes or select the preprogrammed Brown button. Press Start.

3. Add the oil; when hot, use long tongs to add roast. Brown, about 1–2 minutes on each side until it is golden brown. Remove roast to platter and set aside.

4. Add vinegar and wine and scrape bottom with spatula. Add onion and garlic, sauté 1 minute.

5. Add Worcestershire, ketchup, beef base, salt, pepper, and rosemary. Stir in the water and place roast back in pot. Scatter the fingerling potatoes and carrots around roast, if desired.

6. Attach lid and set the pressure valve to Air Tight (closed). Press Cancel and then set the cook time for 50 minutes. Press Start.

7. When the cooking time has elapsed, press the Cancel button to turn off the Keep Warm function.

8. Release the pressure manually, remove lid, and place roast on platter to rest while you make the gravy. To serve, slice roast and serve with gravy (either poured over the roast or on the side) and the veggies.

9. To make the gravy, carefully remove the pressure pot and strain the liquid through a sieve over a bowl or large glass measuring cup. Reserve 3 cups of the liquid.

10. Press the Brown button on the pressure cooker or set cook time to 10 minutes; press Start.

11. Add butter and allow to melt. Sprinkle in flour and mix to form a paste.

12. Slowly add reserved liquid, stirring constantly. Once the mixture begins to boil, turn the pressure cooker to Keep Warm. Simmer until thickened and then stir in cream or milk.

Beef Bourguignon

Prep: 15 min **Ready in:** 1 hour 10 min **Yield:** 6–8 servings

INGREDIENTS

1 tablespoon vegetable oil
4 slices bacon, cut in ½" pieces
1 medium onion, diced
2-pound beef chuck roast, cut in
   1" cubes
3 cloves garlic, crushed
½ teaspoon salt
¼ teaspoon ground pepper
¼ teaspoon ground thyme
1 tablespoon dried parsley
1½ bay leaves
½ cup water
1 cup burgundy wine, divided
4 tablespoons flour
15 pearl onions
15 baby bella or button mushrooms
8 ounces egg noodles
salt and pepper, for serving

1. Place your pressure cooker on a level surface, insert the pressure pot, and plug the unit in.

2. Set Cook Time for 10 minutes or select the preprogrammed Brown button. Press Start.

3. Add the oil; when oil is hot, add the bacon and onion and cook 2–3 minutes or until bacon is beginning to brown. Add the beef and cook another 3 minutes, stirring constantly. Add the garlic, salt, pepper, thyme, parsley, and bay leaves, along with the water and ¾ cup of wine.

4. Attach and lock lid. Set the pressure valve to Air Tight (closed). Press Cancel, set Cook Time to 40 minutes (or press preprogrammed Soup/Stew button), and press Start. When the cooking time has elapsed, release pressure and remove lid.

5. Make a slurry by mixing the remaining ¼ cup wine with the flour. Stir the wine slurry into the pot and add the pearl onions and mushrooms. Replace lid, close valve, and set timer for 4 minutes. When the cooking time has elapsed, let pressure drop naturally.

6. While waiting for the pressure to drop, cook the egg noodles in boiling water as directed on package; drain noodles.

7. Serve the beef, gravy, and mushrooms over a bed of noodles. Offer salt and pepper for extra seasoning.

Barbecue Brisket

Prep Time: 10 min + 8 hours to marinate

Ready in: 1 hour 40 min

 Yield: allow ¼ pound per serving

INGREDIENTS

4–6-pound beef brisket, trimmed of fat
½ teaspoon garlic salt
½ teaspoon onion salt
½ teaspoon celery salt
4-ounce bottle liquid smoke (set aside 3 teaspoons for the sauce)

For the sauce:
2 cups ketchup
½ cup vinegar
½ cup sugar
¼ teaspoon garlic salt
¼ teaspoon onion salt
¼ teaspoon celery salt
3 teaspoons liquid smoke
½ cup Worcestershire sauce

1. Rinse the brisket and pat dry. Place brisket in an airtight container or on a baking sheet with raised edges that can be covered with plastic wrap. Sprinkle with garlic salt, onion salt, and celery salt. Coat all over with liquid smoke. Cover and refrigerate at least 8 hours.

2. Remove the brisket from the refrigerator and pour off any remaining marinade.

3. Place the pressure cooker on a level surface, insert the pot, and plug in the unit.

4. Set Cook Time for 90 minutes. Press Start. Add all of the sauce ingredients and bring to a low boil, stirring often. Let simmer for 3–4 minutes.

5. Place the brisket into the sauce; you may have to cut the brisket into two pieces if it won't fit in the pot. Secure the lid and set the pressure valve to Air Tight (closed).

6. When the cooking time has elapsed, unplug the pressure cooker and let the pressure release naturally until you can safely remove the lid.

7. Remove the brisket to a cutting board and slice thinly against the grain. Serve immediately or return the slices to the pot with the sauce. Serve with sauce.

Baby Back Ribs

Prep Time: 5 min **Ready in:** 1 hour 40 min **Yields:** 4 servings

INGREDIENTS

2 pounds beef (or pork) back or loin ribs
1 tablespoon honey
¼ cup paprika
½ tablespoon salt
1 tablespoon cayenne pepper
1 tablespoon garlic powder
1 tablespoon onion powder
12 ounces ginger ale
½ cup BBQ sauce (homemade or your favorite brand)

TV TIDBIT

Ribs made the Elite brand pressure cooker famous on Home Shopping Network! It's hard to watch the bones easily pulling away from the moist, tender meat without your mouth watering. Then when you see the full 2–3 racks that come out of the cooker . . . well, let's just say that many owners of an Elite pressure cooker will agree that the ribs prompted their purchase!

1. Wash the ribs and pat dry. Rub the meaty side of each rack with ½ tablespoon honey.

2. In a small bowl, mix together the paprika, salt, cayenne, garlic powder, and onion powder. Sprinkle mixture liberally over both racks.

3. Plug in the pressure cooker and place the pot inside. Add ginger ale to the pot.

4. Put the ribs into the cooker by either: **a)** cutting the racks in halves or thirds and laying them down into the pot (recommended if you are planning on crisping them on the grill afterward), or **b)** standing them on their long end by wrapping the first rack around the inside of the pot in a spiral and then spiraling the next rack inside of the first, and so on (recommended if you are cooking more than 2 racks).

5. Pour or baste the BBQ sauce directly onto the ribs. Secure the lid and close the pressure valve to Air Tight (closed).

6. To prepare these for the grill, set Cook Time to 60 minutes. Or, for "fall-off-the-bone" ribs straight from the pressure cooker, set the Cook Time for 80 minutes.

7. After the cooking time has elapsed, turn off and unplug the pressure cooker. The pressure may be released immediately by opening the valve or naturally by waiting until the pressure has dissipated and the lid can safely be removed.

8. Carefully remove ribs from pot and serve immediately with BBQ sauce, or place on a hot grill (or under the broiler) for 5 minutes per side for a crispy, char-grill taste.

All-American Pot Roast with Veggies

Prep Time: 15 min Ready in: 1 hour 20 min

Yield: 1 serving per ¾ pound of meat

INGREDIENTS

2 tablespoons vegetable oil

3–4-pound round roast

½ cup red wine (good quality)

1 medium onion, coarsely chopped

1 clove garlic, minced

1 tablespoon Worcestershire sauce

1 tablespoon ketchup

1 tablespoon beef base (Better Than
  Bouillon® beef base recommended)

1 teaspoon salt

1 teaspoon coarse ground black
  pepper

1 teaspoon celery salt

hot water

½ pound baby carrots

10–12 small red potatoes

4 celery ribs, cut into 1" pieces

1 tablespoon cornstarch

1 cup cold water

1. Place your pressure cooker on a level surface, insert the pressure pot, and plug the unit in.

2. Set Cook Time for 10 minutes or select the preprogrammed Brown button. Press Start.

3. Add the oil; when oil is hot, sear the roast, about 1 minute on each side. Remove roast and set aside.

4. Add the wine and scrape bottom of the pan with spatula. Add onion and garlic, sauté 1 minute. Add Worcestershire, ketchup, beef base, salt, pepper, and celery salt. Place roast back in pan and just cover with hot water. Attach lid and set the pressure valve to Air Tight (closed). Set timer for 50 minutes and press Start.

5. When the cooking time has elapsed, release pressure, remove lid, and add vegetables. Replace lid, set valve to Air Tight (closed), and set the timer for 15 minutes. Release pressure slowly, remove lid, and stir gently. Press Cancel and then set the Cook Time for 3 minutes.

6. Meanwhile, in a small bowl or cup, mix cornstarch and cold water together. When the pot roast begins to boil, pour the cornstarch mixture into liquid around roast.

7. Set the pressure cooker to Keep Warm and simmer slowly until gravy thickens. Serve within the hour with plenty of bread or rolls. Or serve as hot sandwiches.

Spanish Beef

Prep Time: 10 min   **Ready in:** 50 min **Yield:** 6–8 servings

INGREDIENTS

½ cup flour

1 teaspoon salt, divided

1 teaspoon pepper, divided

2-pound sirloin steak, cut into
 6–8 single-serving-sized pieces

2 tablespoons olive oil

2 tablespoons butter

1 large Spanish onion, cut into thin
 rings

2 cloves garlic

¼ cup diced chorizo

¼ cup dry red cooking wine

2 14½-ounce cans diced tomatoes

¼ cup beef broth

1 bay leaf

½ teaspoon thyme

½ cup pimento-stuffed Spanish green
 olives, small

3 cups white or yellow rice, cooked
 according to package directions

1. In a zip-lock baggie, combine flour, ½ teaspoon salt, and ½ teaspoon pepper. Add the steak pieces and toss to coat.

2. Place the pressure cooker on a level surface, insert the pot, and plug in the unit.

3. Press the preprogrammed Brown button or set Cook Time for 5 minutes; press Start. Add the olive oil.

4. When the oil is hot, use tongs to carefully add the coated meat to the oil and fry 1–2 minutes on each side or until lightly browned. (Work in small batches to avoid overcrowding in the pan.) Remove meat and drain on paper towels. Repeat process until all the meat is cooked; add more oil as needed.

5. While the meat drains, add the butter, onion, garlic, and chorizo to the pan. Sauté for 1–2 minutes or until sizzling. Add wine, tomatoes, beef broth, bay leaf, thyme, and remaining salt and pepper. Add the steak back to the mixture.

6. Secure lid, set pressure valve to Air Tight (closed). Press the preprogrammed Beef button or set Cook Time to 30 minutes.

7. After the 30 minutes are up, quickly release the pressure and remove the lid. Use tongs to turn the steaks over and stir the mixture. Add the olives.

8. Reposition the lid, close pressure valve to Air Tight (closed), and set the Cook Time for 5 minutes. Once cooking time has elapsed, release the pressure immediately and serve hot with white or yellow rice!

Beef Lo Mein

Prep Time: 5 min   **Ready in:** 20 min   **Yield:** 4–6 servings

INGREDIENTS

1½ pounds flank steak

1 tablespoon sesame oil

1 medium onion, coarsely chopped

1 medium red bell pepper, coarsely chopped

1 medium green bell pepper, coarsely chopped

1 cup snow peas (optional)

10½-ounce can condensed beef broth

½ cup water

¼ cup low-sodium soy sauce

1 teaspoon ground ginger

2 cloves garlic, chopped

1 pound lo mein noodles or spaghetti (broken in half)

1. Cut flank steak into 3 lengthwise pieces, then into ½" strips.

2. Place the pressure cooker on a level surface, insert the pot, and plug in the unit. Press the preprogrammed Brown button or set Cook Time for 5 minutes and press Start. Add the sesame oil.

3. When the oil is hot, add the meat and quickly sauté 3–4 minutes or until it begins to brown. Add the onions, peppers, and snow peas and stir constantly until they are hot.

4. Add the remaining ingredients (except the noodles) and stir well. When the mixture comes to a boil, stir in the noodles.

5. Quickly secure lid onto the pressure cooker, set pressure valve to Air Tight (closed). Set Cook Time to 7 minutes. After the cooking time has elapsed, immediately release the pressure. Remove the lid and stir.

6. If the noodles aren't done or too much liquid remains, replace lid and turn the cooker to Keep Warm until desired texture is reached.

Chili Mac

Prep Time: 15 min   **Ready in:** 1 hour   **Yield:** 10–12 servings

INGREDIENTS

1½ pounds beef stew meat, or beef chuck, cut into 1" cubes
½ tablespoon kosher salt
2 tablespoons vegetable oil
2 cloves garlic, minced
1 large Spanish onion, chopped
1 cup green bell pepper, diced
¼ cup chili powder (use less or more depending on desired heat)
1 tablespoon ground cumin
15-ounce can diced tomatoes, undrained
8-ounce can tomato sauce
10-ounce can diced tomatoes with chilies, undrained (Ro-tel® recommended)
3 cups low-sodium chicken broth
1 pound small elbow macaroni

COOK'S TIP
For a heartier dish, add a can of Bush's® chili beans in sauce along with the macaroni.

1. Rinse the meat and pat dry with a paper towel; season with the salt.

2. Place the pressure cooker on a level surface, insert the pot, and plug in the unit. Press the preprogrammed Brown button or set the Cook Time to 10 minutes.

3. Add vegetable oil to the pot; when oil is hot, add the meat and cook 4–5 minutes or until well browned. Add the garlic to the meat and cook for 2 minutes.

4. Add the remaining ingredients, except the macaroni, and stir well.

5. Press Cancel and set Cook Time for 15 minutes; press Start. Secure the lid and turn the pressure valve to Air Tight (closed).

6. When cooking time has elapsed, release the pressure manually and open the lid carefully. Stir in the macaroni.

7. Replace the lid, set valve to Air Tight (closed), set Cook Time for 5 minutes, and press Start.

8. When cooking time has elapsed, let pressure release naturally until you are able to remove the lid safely.

9. Stir well. Test the macaroni for doneness. If more time is needed, replace the lid and allow to cook on Keep Warm until tender.

Italian Meatballs in Sauce

Prep Time: 15 min   **Ready in:** 1 hour   **Yield:** 10–12 servings

INGREDIENTS

For the sauce:
3 tablespoons olive oil
1 cup finely chopped onion
2 28-ounce cans crushed tomatoes
2 29-ounce cans tomato sauce
2 tablespoons each dried oregano,
    dried basil, garlic salt, and sugar
1 tablespoon dried thyme
½ teaspoon crushed red pepper flakes
½ teaspoon garlic powder

For the meatballs:
1 pound ground turkey
2 pounds ground extra lean beef
1 small onion, minced
½ small red bell pepper, minced
3 cloves garlic
1 large eggs, beaten
1 tablespoon dried parsley
1 tablespoon dried basil
½ cup panko breadcrumbs
½ cup grated Parmesan cheese

COOK'S TIP
During get-togethers, cover your pressure cooker with a glass lid (or use the pressure lid with the valve set to Exhaust) and use the Keep Warm feature to keep these meatballs piping hot and delicious!

1. Place pressure cooker on a level surface, insert the pot, and plug in the unit. Set Cook Time to 15 minutes; press Start.

2. Add olive oil to the pot. When oil is hot, add the chopped onion and sauté for about 3 minutes. When the onion is tender but not browned, add the rest of the sauce ingredients.

3. Secure the lid and turn pressure valve to Air Tight (closed).

4. When the cooking time has elapsed, turn the Keep Warm feature off and let pressure release naturally.

5. While the sauce is cooking, make the meatballs! In a large bowl, combine the meats. Mix in the minced onion, bell pepper, and garlic. Add the eggs, parsley, basil, breadcrumbs, and cheese. Using your hands, gently incorporate all the ingredients together and form 1½–2" meatballs; set aside.

6. When the pressure is released from the sauce, open the lid carefully and stir the sauce.

7. Carefully drop the meatballs into the sauce, one by one, and stir gently. Replace the lid, set the valve to Air Tight (closed), and set Cook Time to 25 minutes; press Start.

8. When cooking time has elapsed, turn the Keep Warm feature off and let stand for 5 minutes before moving the pressure valve into the Exhaust position.

9. Serve over spaghetti or your favorite pasta—or make hoagies!

Swiss Steak & Onions

Prep Time: 10 min **Ready in:** 50 min **Yield:** 6 servings

INGREDIENTS

1 cup flour
1 teaspoon salt, divided
1 teaspoon ground black pepper,
    divided
2 pounds beef round steak, diced into
    1½"-thick pieces
¼ cup olive oil
1 medium onion, diced
2 cloves garlic, minced
¼ cup carrots, diced
1 bay leaf
1 cup beef broth
2 tablespoons tomato paste
4–5 large onions, sliced into thick
    rings
hot buttered noodles, or steamed
    white rice, for serving

1. In a ziplock baggie, combine flour, ½ teaspoon salt, and ½ teaspoon pepper. Add the steak and shake to coat.

2. Place the pressure cooker on a level surface, insert the pot, and plug in the unit.

3. Press the preprogrammed Brown button or set Cook Time for 5 minutes; press Start. Add the olive oil.

4. When the oil is hot, add the coated meat to the pan and fry 1–2 minutes on each side or until lightly browned. Work in small batches to avoid overcrowding the pan. Remove meat and drain on paper towels. Repeat process until all the meat is cooked; add more oil as needed.

5. After the meat has been removed, add the onion, garlic, carrots, bay leaf, and remaining salt and pepper to the pan.

6. Sauté for just 1 minute and then add the beef broth, tomato paste, and the browned steak pieces.

7. Secure lid onto the pressure cooker and set pressure valve to Air Tight (closed).

8. Set Cook Time to 30 minutes. When the cooking time has elapsed, let the pressure release naturally for 5 minutes and then release remaining pressure manually.

9. Stir the mixture and add the onion rings to the top. Reposition the lid and set the timer for 5 minutes. Once cooking time has elapsed, press Cancel to turn off the Keep Warm feature and allow cooker to cool naturally until you can safely remove the lid.

10. Serve with hot buttered noodles or steamed white rice.

Sloppy Joes

Prep Time: 5 min   **Ready in:** 40 min   **Yield:** 6–8 sandwiches

INGREDIENTS

2 tablespoons olive oil
1 large onion, diced
1 clove garlic, minced
1½ pounds lean ground beef
¾ cup beef broth
6-ounce can tomato paste
2 tablespoons light brown sugar
1 teaspoon salt
½ teaspoon chili powder
1 tablespoon Worcestershire sauce
pinch of crushed red pepper flakes

1. Place the pressure cooker on a level surface, insert the pot, and plug in the unit.

2. Press the preprogrammed Brown button or set Cook Time for 5 minutes; press Start. Add the olive oil.

3. When the oil is hot, add the onion and garlic. Sauté about 3 minutes and then add the ground beef.

4. Cook for 2 minutes, stirring well to break up the meat. If the meat is fatty, carefully remove pot and pour the meat into a colander to strain the grease, then return to pot and place in the pressure cooker again. Add the remaining ingredients and stir well.

5. Secure the lid in place and set the pressure valve to Air Tight (closed). Press Cancel and then select the preprogrammed Beef button or set the Cook Time to 30 minutes.

6. When cooking time has elapsed, unplug the pressure cooker and release pressure, manually or naturally, until lid can safely be removed.

7. Stir well and serve hot on rolls or buns.

Beef & Mushroom Stroganoff

Prep Time: 5 min **Ready in:** 35 min **Yield:** 6–8 servings

INGREDIENTS

1 tablespoon vegetable oil
2 tablespoons butter, divided
2-pound beef tenderloin, trimmed and
    cut into 1" pieces
1 large onion, diced
1 pound white mushrooms, sliced
1 clove garlic, minced
1 teaspoon salt
1 tablespoon Worcestershire sauce
1 tablespoon flour
½ cup white wine
3 cups beef stock
16-ounce package wide egg noodles
1 cup sour cream

1. Place the pressure cooker on a level surface, insert the pot, and plug in the unit.

2. Press the preprogrammed Beef button or set Cook Time for 15 minutes; press Start. Add the oil and 1 tablespoon of the butter. When pot is hot, add the beef and cook until the juices run. Carefully remove pot, drain beef into a colander, wipe out the pot, and place back in the cooker.

3. Add the remaining butter to the pot. When pot is hot, add the onion, mushrooms, and garlic. Add in the salt and the Worcestershire sauce. Sauté about 3 minutes and then sprinkle in the flour; cook about 1 minute and then slowly pour in the wine and stir until bubbly.

4. Return the beef to the pot and add the beef stock; stir well. Attach the lid and set the pressure valve to Air Tight (closed). When cooking time has elapsed, press Cancel and wait 7 minutes before releasing the pressure manually.

5. Open lid and stir well. Add noodles. Attach the lid and set the pressure valve to Air Tight (closed).

6. Set Cook Time for 5 minutes. Press Start.

7. When cooking time has elapsed, unplug the pressure cooker and release pressure, manually or naturally, until lid can safely be removed.

8. Stir in the sour cream. Heat through, toss, and serve.

Stuffed Peppers

Prep Time: 10 min   **Ready in:** 40 min   **Yield:** 5–6 servings

INGREDIENTS

1¼ pounds lean ground beef

1 cup onion, finely chopped

½ teaspoon dried oregano

1 teaspoon dried basil

½ teaspoon garlic powder

1 teaspoon garlic salt

1 teaspoon dried thyme

1½ cups spaghetti sauce, or tomato sauce, or tomato soup, divided

2 cups long grain rice

3¾ cups water, divided

5 large bell peppers, any color

2–3 slices of American cheese

1. Place pressure cooker on a level surface, insert the pot, and plug in the unit. Press preprogrammed Rice button or set cook time to 12 minutes; press Start.

2. Add the ground beef and cook until browned. Add the onion and sauté for another 2 minutes. When the onion is tender, stir in the seasonings and ½ cup of the tomato sauce.

3. Add rice and 2¾ cups water; stir well. Secure the lid, turn pressure valve to Air Tight (closed).

4. When the cooking time has elapsed, wait 5–7 minutes before releasing the pressure manually.

5. While the mixture is cooking, prepare the peppers. First, stand the peppers upright and trim the bottom as necessary to keep the pepper from toppling over while cooking. Next, remove the top of the pepper and hollow out the membranes and seeds; discard.

6. When pressure is released, remove the lid carefully and stir the mixture well. Stuff the peppers with beef-rice mixture; place on plate and set aside.

7. Wash, rinse, and dry the pot; return to base. Pour the remaining 1 cup water into the bottom of the cooker.

8. Place the peppers into the pot. Attach the lid and set the exhaust valve to Air Tight (closed). Set Cook Time to 5 minutes or press the preprogrammed Vegetable button.

9. When cooking time has elapsed, wait 3–5 minutes before releasing the pressure. Remove the lid carefully.

10. Spoon the remaining 1 cup spaghetti sauce evenly over the stuffed peppers and top with cheese.

11. Return lid to cooker but leave valve on Exhaust. Let rest 5 minutes before serving. While the cheese is melting, reheat any remaining meat and rice mixture and serve alongside the stuffed peppers.

Osso Buco

Prep Time: 15 min   **Ready in:** 1 hour   **Yield:** 1 serving per ⅓ pound of meat

INGREDIENTS

½ cup flour

1 teaspoon salt

1 teaspoon paprika

3–4 pounds veal shanks (2–3" thick)

½ cup olive oil

⅓ cup onion, chopped

½ cup carrots, chopped

½ red bell pepper, seeds and membrane removed, chopped

2 cloves garlic, chopped

¾ cup white wine (Sauvignon Blanc recommended)

3 sprigs thyme

3–4 small celery stalks with leaves attached

2 cups hot water

1½ tablespoons beef base (Better Than Bouillon® beef base recommended)

15 ounces tomato sauce

2 bay leaves

4 cups wide egg noodles, cooked to desired texture

1. Place the flour, salt, and paprika into a ziplock baggie and shake together. Add veal shanks to the baggie and shake to coat well. Set aside.

2. Place pot inside pressure cooker, plug in the pressure cooker, select the preprogrammed Brown button, or set Cook Time to 10 minutes; press Start. Add the olive oil to the pan. When the oil is hot, use tongs to lower the veal shanks into the pot. Brown 2–3 minutes on each side and then remove to a plate.

3. Add the onion, carrots, and bell pepper to the pot and sauté for about 1 minute. Add the garlic, stir well, and then add the wine. Bring to a boil. Add the thyme and celery stalks and let the mixture cook for 2–3 minutes.

4. Stir in the water, beef base, tomato sauce, and bay leaves. Use the tongs to lower each shank into the liquid, turning over a couple of times to coat with the liquid. Secure the lid and set the pressure valve to Air Tight (closed). Press Cancel, set the Cook Time to for 45 minutes, and press Start.

5. When the cooking time has elapsed, press the Stop button to cancel the Keep Warm function. Release the pressure manually, open lid, and stir. Serve with the egg noodles and offer the extra sauce on the side.

Pork Chops & Applesauce

Prep Time: 5 min **Ready in:** 30 min **Yield:** 4 servings

INGREDIENTS

4 medium boneless pork loin chops, about ½" thick
1 teaspoon salt
1 teaspoon coarse ground pepper
3 tablespoons vegetable oil
3 tablespoons butter
1 shallot, finely chopped
1 clove garlic, minced
2 teaspoons balsamic vinegar
1 tablespoon dried rosemary
1 heaping tablespoon light brown sugar
1¼ cups apple cider
2 large granny smith apples, peeled, cored and cut into thick slices

1. Rinse pork chops and pat dry with paper towels. Sprinkle with salt and pepper.

2. Place pressure cooker on a level surface, insert the pan, and plug in the unit. Select the Browning feature or set Cook Time to 8 minutes. Add the oil.

3. When oil is hot, brown the chops on both sides and then drain on paper towels.

4. Carefully pour off about half of the oil. Add butter, shallots, and garlic; cook gently for about 1 minute. Add the vinegar and scrape the bottom of the pan with a spatula.

5. Add the rosemary, brown sugar, and apple cider; stir well. Place chops back in pot.

6. Attach lid and set pressure valve to Air Tight (closed). Press Cancel and set Cook Time for 10 minutes (or press the preprogrammed Pork button); press Start.

7. When cooking time has elapsed, release pressure and remove lid carefully. Turn the chops over and top with the apple slices. Reattach lid, close the regulator valve, and set Cook Time for 4 minutes. Press Start.

8. When cooking time has elapsed, release pressure and carefully remove lid.

9. Remove the chops to a plate; cover with foil to keep warm. To serve the apples, they can be further mashed, stirred into the liquid, or removed with a slotted spoon and served on the chops.

Apricot Pork Roast

Prep Time: 10 min   **Ready in:** 45 min   **Yield:** 10–12 servings

INGREDIENTS

2½–3½-pound pork loin roast
1½ teaspoons salt
½ teaspoon coarse ground black
    pepper
1 tablespoon fresh rosemary, chopped
2 tablespoons Dijon mustard
1 tablespoon vegetable oil
1 cup dried apricots, sliced
1 tablespoon honey
1 tablespoon brown sugar
1 cup + 2 tablespoons water, divided
2 tablespoons corn starch

COOK'S TIP

This recipe will result in a sliceable roast. If you prefer a shreddable roast, increase the cooking time to 45 minutes.

1. Place your pressure cooker on a level surface, insert the pot, and plug the unit in.

2. Rinse pork roast and pat dry with paper towels. Make a paste with the salt, pepper, rosemary, and mustard; rub the paste on the roast.

3. Set cook time to 30 minutes (or press Pork button) and press Start. Add oil.

4. When oil is hot, use tongs to lower the roast into the pot. Sear the edges of the roast on all sides, using the tongs to turn (about 1–2 minutes on each side).

5. Mix the apricot slices, honey, and brown sugar into 1 cup of water; pour over the top of the roast in the pot.

6. Attach the lid and set the pressure control to Air Tight (closed).

7. When cooking time has elapsed, release the pressure manually by opening the pressure control valve to exhaust.

8. Once the pressure has been released, open the lid carefully and remove roast to a cutting board.

9. Press any preprogrammed button or set Cook Time to 5 minutes.

10. Mix 2 tablespoons water with the corn starch to make a slurry. When the liquid in the pot begins to boil, stir in the slurry and turn off the pressure cooker.

11. Serve by slicing the roast and topping with the apricot mixture.

Cherry Port–Glazed Pork Roast

Prep Time: 10 min   **Ready in:** 45 min   **Yield:** 10–12 servings

INGREDIENTS

2½–3½-pound pork loin roast

1½ teaspoons salt

1 teaspoon garlic powder

½ teaspoon coarse ground black pepper

1 tablespoon fresh thyme or rosemary, chopped

1 tablespoon olive oil

¾ cup ruby port

½ cup cherry pie filling

½ cup water + 2 tablespoons water, divided

2 tablespoons corn starch

COOK'S TIP

This recipe will result in a sliceable roast. If you prefer a shreddable roast, increase the cooking time to 45 minutes.

1. Place your pressure cooker on a level surface, insert the pot, and plug the unit in.

2. Rinse pork roast and pat dry with paper towels. Combine the salt, garlic powder, pepper, and fresh thyme or rosemary; sprinkle evenly on the roast and rub in well.

3. Set Cook Time to 25 minutes (or press Pork button) and press Start. Add olive oil.

4. When oil is hot, use tongs to lower the roast into the pot. Sear the edges of the roast on all sides, using the tongs to turn (about 1–2 minutes on each side).

5. Pour the port over the roast. Let the port wine cook down 5 minutes as you continue to turn the pork over.

6. Mix pie filling into ½ cup water; pour over the top of the roast in the pot.

7. Attach the lid and set the pressure control to Air Tight (closed).

8. When cooking time has elapsed, release the pressure manually by opening the pressure control valve to exhaust.

9. Once the pressure has been released, open the lid carefully and remove roast to a cutting board.

10. Press any preprogrammed button or set Cook Time to 5 minutes.

11. Mix 2 tablespoons water with the corn starch to make a slurry. When the liquid in the pot begins to boil, stir in the slurry and turn off the pressure cooker.

12. Serve by slicing the roast and topping with the cherry mixture.

Sweet 'n' Sour Pork Roast

Prep Time: 5 min   **Ready in:** 1 hour 15 min   Yield: allow ¼ pound per serving

INGREDIENTS

3–4-pound boneless pork loin roast
1 teaspoon salt
1 teaspoon pepper
1 cup water
1 large onion, cut into large
   bite-sized chunky pieces
1 green bell pepper, cut into large
   bite-sized chunky pieces
1 red bell pepper, cut into large
   bite-sized chunky pieces
20-ounce can pineapple chunks, drain
   but save the liquid
1 tablespoon corn starch
9 ounces sweet 'n' sour sauce
   (World Harbors® Maui
   Mountain teriyaki recommended)
Cooked white rice, for serving

1. Place pressure cooker on a level surface, insert the pot, and plug in the unit.

2. Rinse the roast and pat dry with paper towels. Sprinkle the roast with salt and pepper and place into the pressure cooker pot with 1 cup water.

3. Secure lid and set the pressure valve to Air Tight (closed). Press the preprogrammed Pork button or set Cook Time to 30 minutes.

4. When the cook time has elapsed, press Cancel to turn off the machine. Place a cold damp towel over the top and wait 5 minutes. Allow pressure to drop (about 10 minutes) or gently toggle the pressure gauge and quick release the pressure until you can safely remove the lid.

5. Place the roast on a plate and drain the liquid from the pot. Return the roast to the pot and add the onion, bell peppers, and drained pineapple chunks.

6. In a medium bowl, whisk together 2 tablespoons of the pineapple juice and the corn starch to make a slurry. Whisk in the remaining pineapple juice and the sweet 'n' sour sauce. Pour mixture over the roast and veggies.

7. Reattach lid, set valve to Air Tight (closed), and press the preprogrammed Pork button or set Cook Time to 30 minutes.

8. When the cooker switches to Keep Warm, follow the same method above to release the pressure and remove the lid.

9. Slice and serve with white rice.

Mojo Pork

Prep Time: 5 min Ready in: 17 min **Yield:** 1 chop per serving

INGREDIENTS

3-pound Boston butt roast
1 tablespoon olive oil
1 sweet onion, coarsely chopped
¾ cup mojo sauce, store bought or homemade (instructions provided)
¼ cup water
Cooked white rice, for serving

For the mojo sauce:
1 cup extra virgin olive oil
1 teaspoon ground cumin
1 teaspoon salt
4 tablespoons minced garlic
6 tablespoons lime juice
6 tablespoons orange juice
2 teaspoons oregano leaves
2 teaspoons lemon juice

COOK'S TIP

This dish is traditionally served with white or yellow rice, black beans, and chopped onion. Complete the meal with fried plantains and sangria, and you'll think you're in Cuba!

1. Whisk together all the ingredients for the mojo sauce; set aside until ready to use.

2. Place your pressure cooker on a level surface, insert the pot, and plug the unit in.

3. Rinse roast and pat dry with paper towels; set aside.

4. Set Cook Time to 70 minutes and press Start. Add 1 tablespoon olive oil.

5. When oil is hot, add onion. Brown for 2–3 minutes or until onion softens.

6. Using tongs, lower roast carefully into the pot. Add mojo sauce and water. Use the tongs to turn the roast in the liquid until all sides are coated.

7. Attach the lid and set the pressure control to Air Tight (closed).

8. When cooking time has elapsed, release the pressure manually by opening the pressure control valve to exhaust.

9. Once the pressure has been released, open the lid carefully and remove roast to a cutting board.

10. Use two forks to shred the pork and then place back into the pot; toss with the sauce and onions.

11. Close lid, leave the valve on Exhaust, and use the Keep Warm function until ready to serve. Serve with warm white rice.

Barbecue Pork Pull-Apart

Prep Time: 5 min   Ready in: 1 hour 25 min   **Yield:** 12 servings or sandwiches

INGREDIENTS

3½-pound pork shoulder blade roast, rinsed and patted dry

16 ounces beer

1 cup water

1 tablespoon liquid smoke

1 teaspoon onion salt

1 teaspoon Kosher salt

1 teaspoon coarse ground pepper

18 ounces barbecue sauce (your favorite brand)

dill pickle slices, for serving (optional)

onion, thinly sliced, for serving (optional)

TV TIDBIT

When showing this delicious dish on live TV, it's always a little scary for the on-air guest when they are first "pulling" the roast. There's the chance of a big blob of fat, a string that was forgotten to be removed, or worse, a super tough piece of meat that just won't shred! Although the pressure cooker makes this virtually impossible to mess up, it can (and does) happen occasionally. If you were unlucky enough to get an overly lean, tough cut of meat, try it again . . . it's usually perfect!

1. Rinse roast and pat dry with paper towels. Set aside.

2. Place pressure cooker on a level surface, insert the pot, and plug in the unit. Add beer, water, liquid smoke, onion salt, Kosher salt, and pepper to the pot. Stir and allow bubbles to subside. Add the pork roast.

3. Secure lid, set the pressure valve to Air Tight (closed), and set timer for 1 hour 15 minutes. Press Start.

4. When cook time has elapsed, release pressure. Remove roast from pan and place onto a cutting board. Discard liquid from the pot.

5. Remove bone and any large fat portions from roast; discard. Using two large forks, shred meat, or chop if you prefer.

6. Serve on buns as is, or with a drizzle of barbecue sauce, dill pickle slices, and thinly sliced onion! To serve later, return meat to pan and stir in barbecue sauce, mixing well; set the pressure cooker to Keep Warm; cover, leaving pressure valve at Exhaust, and serve when desired (if it's going to be in the pot for a while, you may need to add additional barbeue sauce or ¼ cup water to keep the meat moist until you are ready to serve).

Blackberry Balsamic Pork Chops

Prep Time: 5 min **Ready in:** 20 min **Yield:** 1 chop per serving

INGREDIENTS

1–4 center-cut pork loin chops, bone-in, ¾" thick
½ teaspoon salt
½ teaspoon pepper
1 tablespoon fresh rosemary, chopped
1 tablespoon olive oil
1 teaspoon Dijon mustard
¾ cup + 2 tablespoons water, divided
2½ tablespoons balsamic vinegar
2 teaspoons corn starch
⅔ cup fresh blackberries
(about 20 berries)

1. Rinse pork chops and pat dry with paper towels. Lightly season both sides with salt, pepper, and rosemary. Set aside.

2. Place your pressure cooker on a level surface, insert the pressure pot, and plug the unit in. Set Cook Time to 10 minutes and press Start. Add olive oil to the pot.

3. When oil is hot, add pork chops. Cook 2–3 minutes on each side or until they begin to brown.

4. While pork chops are browning, stir the Dijon mustard into ¾ cup water.

5. When pork chops have browned, add the balsamic vinegar to the pot, followed by the mustard-water mixture. Attach the lid of your pressure cooker and set the pressure control to Air Tight (closed).

6. When cooking time has elapsed, release the pressure manually by opening the pressure control valve to exhaust. Open the lid carefully, remove pork chops to a plate, and cover them with foil to keep warm.

7. Press the Cancel button and reset Cook Time to 4 minutes; press Start.

8. In a small bowl, whisk together 2 tablespoons water with the corn starch to make a slurry. When the mixture in the pot begins to boil, add the slurry and blackberries. Stir well.

9. Let sauce cook for 2–3 minutes or until thickened. Serve immediately over pork chops.

Ginger Pork Stir Fry

Prep Time: 10 min **Ready in:** 30 min **Yield:** 4–6 servings

INGREDIENTS

10-ounce pork loin roast, trimmed
1½ teaspoons salt
½ teaspoon paprika
1 tablespoon olive oil
2 teaspoons sesame oil
1 medium orange bell pepper, thinly sliced
1 cup snow peas
½ cup julienned celery
1 tablespoon minced and peeled fresh ginger
2 cups chicken broth
3 tablespoons rice vinegar
1 tablespoon soy sauce
2 teaspoons sugar
1 teaspoon chili garlic sauce
8 ounces angel hair pasta, or thin spaghetti

TV TIDBIT

When making dishes like this on TV, the snow peas and the orange pepper would not be cooked but rather tossed in raw at the end to show off fresh, vibrant color!

1. Rinse pork roast and pat dry with paper towels. Cut into bite-sized pieces and toss with the salt and paprika.

2. Place your pressure cooker on a level surface, insert the pot, and plug the unit in. Set Cook Time to 7 minutes (or press Pork button and adjust time) and press Start. Add olive oil.

3. When oil is hot, add pork cubes. Sear about 1–2 minutes on each side, using tongs to turn the pork

4. Remove pork to a plate. Add the sesame oil to the pot, then add the bell pepper, snow peas, celery, and ginger.

5. Return pork to pot and stir fry for about 1 minute. Carefully add the chicken broth, rice vinegar, soy sauce, sugar, and chili garlic sauce. Stir well.

6. Break the pasta in half and add it to the pot. Use a fork to separate the noodles.

7. Attach the lid and set the pressure control to Air Tight (closed).

8. When cooking time has elapsed, release the pressure manually by opening the pressure control valve to exhaust.

9. Once the pressure has been released, open the lid carefully. Toss contents to distribute sauce evenly. Serve immediately.

Pork Chops with Olives

Prep Time: 7 min   **Ready in:** 13 min   **Yield:** 1 chop per serving

INGREDIENTS

1–4 center-cut pork loin chops, bone-in, ¾" thick

½ teaspoon salt

½ teaspoon pepper

1 tablespoon olive oil

¼ cup onions, diced

1 large clove of garlic, minced

14½-ounce can petite diced tomatoes

2 bay leaves

½ cup small green pimento-stuffed olives, chopped

COOK'S TIP
Serve with white or yellow rice and a cold green salad.

1. Rinse pork chops and pat dry with paper towels. Lightly season both sides with salt and pepper.

2. Place your pressure cooker on a level surface, insert the pot, and plug the unit in. Set Cook Time to 10 minutes and press Start. Add olive oil to the pot.

3. When oil is hot, add onions. Cook for minute, stirring constantly.

4. Add pork chops. Cook for 2 minutes on one side, then turn the pork chops over.

5. Add minced garlic to the sizzling onions; stir well and cook another 2 minutes.

6. Add tomatoes, bay leaves, and olives; stir gently.

7. Attach the lid and set the pressure control to Air Tight (closed).

8. When cooking time has elapsed, release the pressure manually by opening the pressure control valve to exhaust. Open lid carefully and serve immediately.

Spicy Lamb Meatballs

Prep Time: 20 min   **Ready in:** 45 min   **Yield:** 10–20 servings

INGREDIENTS

For the yogurt sauce:
1 cup Greek yogurt
½ cup English cucumber, peeled, seeded, finely chopped
½ teaspoon garlic powder
⅓ cup fresh mint, chopped

For the meatballs:
1½ pounds ground lean lamb
1 small white onion, minced
1 clove garlic, minced
½ small red bell pepper, minced
1½ teaspoons ground cumin
1 teaspoon ground coriander
⅓ cup fresh parsley, minced
1 jalapeño, seeds and membrane removed, minced
zest and juice of 1 lemon
1 large egg, beaten
½ cup breadcrumbs
olive oil
1 cup water

1. In a bowl or container, stir together ingredients for yogurt sauce. Store in refrigerator until ready to serve.

2. In a large bowl, combine ground lamb, onion, garlic, bell pepper, cumin, coriander, parsley, jalapeño, and lemon (zest and juice). Add the eggs and breadcrumbs. Using your hands, gently incorporate all the ingredients together and then form 1½–2" inch meatballs; set aside.

3. Place pressure cooker on a level surface, insert the pot and plug in. Set Cook Time to 15 minutes; press Start. Add olive oil to the pot (enough to cover the bottom). When oil is hot, add a single layer of meatballs to the bottom of the pan. Brown on all sides, using long tongs to turn the meatballs. Remove to a paper towel. Repeat in batches until all meatballs have been browned, adding a little more olive oil as needed.

4. When the last batch is finished, pour in the water and scrape the bottom of the pan to loosen any stuck-on bits. Put the meatballs back into the cooker. Secure the lid, turn pressure valve to Air Tight (closed). Press Meat, or set Cook Time to 20 minutes.

5. When the cooking time has elapsed, turn off the Keep Warm feature and let pressure release naturally.

6. Serve with the yogurt sauce as an appetizer or as an entrée.

Chicken & Turkey

Chicken & Turkey

SLOW COOK FAST!
Whole chickens cook deliciously in a fraction of the time
and yield that fall-off-the-bone tenderness!

Poultry Cooking Times

Poultry	Brown?	Minimum Liquid	Minimum Cook Time (minutes)	Release Method
Chicken breast, bone-in (up to 3 lbs. of ⅓ lb. individual pieces)	yes	1 cup	7	natural
Chicken breast, boneless (up to 3 lbs. of ⅓ lb. individual pieces)	yes	1 cup	6	natural
Chicken breast, boneless strips, tenders	yes	½ cup	4	quick
Chicken livers	no	1 cup	3	quick
Chicken, ground meat	yes	¾ cup	4	quick
Chicken legs or thighs, bone-in (up to 3 lbs.)	yes	¾ cup	7	quick
Chicken legs or thighs, boneless (up to 3 lbs.)	yes	¾ cup	6	quick
Chicken sausage, Italian, Polish, kielbasa (steam on rack)	yes	¾ cup	8	quick
Chicken wings	no	¾ cup	6	quick
Chicken, whole (not stuffed, 2–3 lbs.)	no	1 cup	18–20	natural
Chicken, whole (not stuffed, 3–4 lbs.)	no	1 cup	20–25	natural
Cornish hen, whole	no	¾ cup	8–10	natural
Duck, cut into pieces (use rack)	yes	¾ cup	8–10	natural
Duck, whole (3–4 lbs.) (use rack)	yes	1 cup	25–30	natural
Turkey breast, boneless (3 lbs.)	no	1 cup	20–22	natural
Turkey breast, bone-in (3–4 lbs.)	no	1 cup	20–25	natural
Turkey breast, ground meat	no	¾ cup	8–10	natural
Turkey legs, up to 6	yes	¾ cup	12	natural
Turkey sausage, Italian, Polish, kielbasa (steam on rack)	yes	¾ cup	8	natural

Spanish Chicken

Prep Time: 5 min **Ready in:** 40 min **Yield:** 4 servings

INGREDIENTS

2 tablespoons olive oil

1 medium yellow onion, sliced into thick rings

3 cloves garlic, minced

28-ounce can crushed tomatoes

¼ teaspoon salt

1 bay leaf

10 large Spanish olives, cut in half

4 frozen boneless, skinless chicken breasts (about 1–1⅓ pounds)

TV TIDBIT

Doing a frozen chicken demo for TV shopping presentations of the Elite pressure cooker has been popular for many years because it really works! This recipe uses tomatoes and is served over rice, but you can vary it by using salsa and serving chicken tacos, or using cream of mushroom soup and serving over noodles. The possibilities are endless! Have fun and make up your own "demos"!

COOK'S TIP

Save a little time by substituting thawed chicken. The cook time will automatically be reduced by about 5–8 minutes because the cooker will come to pressure faster!

1. Place your pressure cooker on a level surface, insert the pot, and plug the unit in.

2. Set Cook Time to 15 minutes or select the preprogrammed Chicken button; press Start. Add the olive oil.

3. When oil is hot, add the onion and garlic. Sauté for 1–2 minutes, then stir in the tomatoes, salt, bay leaf, and olives.

4. Use tongs to place frozen chicken into the sauce.

5. Attach the lid and turn the pressure valve to Air Tight (closed).

6. When the machine switches to Keep Warm, turn the machine off. Place a cold damp towel over the top and wait 5 minutes. Allow pressure to drop (about 10 minutes), or gently toggle the pressure gauge and quick-release the pressure until you can safely remove the lid.

COOK'S TIP
Serve with yellow or white rice.

Chicken with Raspberry Glaze

Prep Time: 10 min   **Ready in:** 30 min   **Yield:** 4–6 servings

INGREDIENTS

4 skinless, boneless chicken breast
   halves
½ teaspoon salt
¼ teaspoon pepper
2 tablespoons butter, divided
2 tablespoons vegetable oil, divided
6 scallions, chopped
⅓ cup raspberry vinegar
½ cup chicken broth
1 tablespoon Dijon mustard
⅓ cup heavy cream
1 cup fresh or frozen raspberries

1. Rinse chicken and pat dry with paper towels. Season with salt and pepper.

2. Place your pressure cooker on a level surface, insert the pot, and plug the unit in. Set Cook Time to 15 minutes or press the preprogrammed Chicken button and adjust time from there. Press Start.

3. Add 1 tablespoon butter and 1 tablespoon vegetable oil to the pot. When hot, add the chicken, without overlapping, and cook, turning once, until both sides are lightly browned (3–4 minutes). Remove to a plate.

4. Add the remaining butter and oil. Sauté the scallions for 1–2 minutes until soft and fragrant.

5. Stir in the raspberry vinegar, chicken broth, and mustard. Return the chicken to the pot. Attach the lid and turn the pressure valve to Air Tight (closed).

6. When the Cook Time has elapsed, release the pressure manually. Open the lid carefully. Remove chicken to a plate, cover with foil, and set aside.

7. The cooker should be on Keep Warm; if not, set Cook Time to 5 minutes.

8. Bring liquid to a boil and stir in the heavy cream. Simmer 2–3 minutes, until sauce slightly thickens.

9. Return chicken to pan. Add the raspberries and stir gently. Cook until heated through, about 1 minute.

10. To serve, arrange the chicken on a warm platter and pour the sauce over all.

Easy Chicken 'n' Dumplings

Prep Time: 20 min   **Ready in:** 35 min   **Yield:** 4–6 servings

INGREDIENTS
1–1½ pounds boneless, skinless
    chicken breasts
½ teaspoon salt
¼ teaspoon pepper
2 7½-ounce cans of biscuits
3 tablespoons butter
½ cup diced carrots
¼ cup diced celery
¼ cup flour
4 cups chicken broth
¼ teaspoon poultry seasoning

COOK'S TIP
If you have extra time, prepare a
whole chicken and use the shredded
meat rather than the breasts.
It gives the dish an extra depth
of flavor that you can't get from
breasts alone.

NEED TO FEED A CROWD?
You can double or triple this recipe
as needed.

1. Rinse chicken and pat dry with paper towels. Cut chicken into bite-sized pieces. Sprinkle with salt and pepper and set aside.

2. Open the cans of biscuits and lay them out onto a cutting board. Press each biscuit semiflat and then cut into 1"-wide strips (about 4 strips per biscuit). Set aside.

3. Place your pressure cooker on a level surface and plug the unit in. Set Cook Time to 20 minutes or select the Chicken setting; press Start.

4. When the pot begins to heat up, add butter. Stir in the carrots and celery and cook until lightly browned.

5. Add the flour and stir in well. Cook for 1–2 minutes or until it is beginning to brown. If the flour is not quite moist enough, add a little chicken broth at this time.

6. Stir in the chicken broth, cubed chicken breasts, and poultry seasoning.

7. Using a spoon, slowly drop the canned biscuits into the mixture, gently pushing biscuits into broth so that each biscuit piece has been coated.

8. Attach the lid and set the pressure valve to Air Tight (closed). When the pressure cooker switches to Keep Warm, unplug the machine and let the pressure slowly drop until no pressure remains.

9. Open lid, stir well, close the lid, and let rest 5 minutes before serving.

Chicken 'n' Rice

Prep Time: 5 min   **Ready in:** 25 min   **Yield:** 4 servings

INGREDIENTS

3 tablespoons vegetable oil

½ medium onion, minced

1 cup minced baby carrots

6 cups chicken broth

1 teaspoon salt

½ teaspoon freshly ground black pepper

¼ teaspoon garlic powder

1½ pounds boneless skinless chicken breast, cut into bite-sized pieces

3 cups long grain white rice

COOK'S TIP
To use brown rice for this recipe, adjust the Cook Time to 16 minutes or choose the Brown Rice preprogrammed button.

1. Place your pressure cooker on a level surface, insert the pot, and plug the unit in.

2. Set cook time to 12 minutes or select the preprogrammed Rice button; press Start. Add oil to pot.

3. When oil is hot, add the onion and sauté for 1–2 minutes. Add the carrots and sauté another 2 minutes.

4. Add the broth, salt, pepper, garlic powder, and chicken pieces and bring to a boil.

5. Stir in the rice. Attach the lid and turn the pressure valve to Air Tight (closed).

6. When the machine switches to Keep Warm, press Cancel to turn the machine off.

7. Allow pressure to drop naturally for about 10 minutes, or gently toggle the pressure gauge and quick-release the remaining pressure until you can safely remove the lid. Serve immediately.

Buffalo-Style Chicken Wings

Prep Time: 5 min   **Ready in:** 25 min   **Yield:** ~6 entrée portions, or ~15 appetizer portions

INGREDIENTS

5 pounds chicken wings (I buy the frozen sectioned wings and do not use the tips.)
1–2 teaspoons salt
12-ounce bottle wing sauce (I like Crystal®, but you can use your favorite!)

NEED TO FEED A CROWD?

Multiply this recipe to make as many wings as you need! For every quart your cooker can hold, estimate about 1½ pounds chicken wings. For example, a 4-quart cooker easily holds 6 pounds of wings. A 12-quart cooker can make 20 pounds of chicken wings in one go!

COOK'S TIP

These wings are even better if you crisp them up a bit before serving! After pressure cooking, arrange wings in a single layer on a nonstick pan. Turn your oven's broiler to "high." Place wings under the broiler on a middle rack. Cook 3–5 minutes or until they are beginning to crisp. Turn wings over and brown the other side. Baste with wing sauce as desired.

1. Place your pressure cooker on a level surface, insert the pot, and plug the unit in.

2. Place the wings in a colander, 5 pounds at a time, and with cold water running over them, use your hands to wash each one. Place them on a cookie sheet lined with paper towels and pat dry.

3. Sprinkle lightly with salt and place into the cooker. Pour ½ cup wing sauce over the wings and use your hands again to mix well. (If making a larger batch, repeat Steps 1–3 until you have as many wings in the pot as you would like.)

4. Set Cook Time for 15 minutes and press Start. Attach the lid and set the exhaust valve to the Air Tight (closed) position and let cook.

5. When the cooking time has elapsed, unplug or remove from heat and let the cooker rest for 5 minutes before releasing the pressure manually. Open the lid carefully.

6. If you are cooking only 5 pounds of wings, carefully remove the pot and drain the liquid from the wings; spread wings onto a nonstick cookie sheet. If you have a full pot of wings, use a slotted spoon to place the wings on the cookie sheet. (Do NOT try to drain an entire pot of wings: it is heavy, and the steam will burn you!)

7. Serve the wings hot, with the remaining wing sauce on a platter with celery sticks and either ranch or bleu cheese dressing.

Chicken Tacos

Prep Time: 15 min   **Ready in:** 25 min   **Yield:** 10–12 servings

INGREDIENTS

2 cups chicken broth

1½ teaspoons cumin, divided

½ teaspoon onion salt

6 6-ounce frozen or thawed boneless
  skinless chicken breast halves
  (about 2 pounds)

1 tablespoon olive oil

1 medium onion, diced

¼ teaspoon cayenne pepper

4-ounce can chopped green chilies

5½-ounce can spicy V8® juice

12 soft tortillas, or 12 hard taco shells
  (or combo of both!)

Optional toppings: lettuce, shredded
  cheddar or Jack cheese, sour
  cream, salsa, sliced jalapeños

1. Place your pressure cooker on a level surface, insert the pot, and plug the unit in.

2. Set Cook Time to 20 minutes or select the preprogrammed Chicken button; press Start.

3. Pour the chicken broth into the pot and stir in 1 teaspoon cumin and the onion salt; bring to a boil.

4. Use tongs to add the chicken breasts. Attach the lid and turn the pressure valve to Air Tight (closed).

5. When the cooking time has elapsed, allow pressure to release naturally until no pressure remains and you can open the lid. Remove the chicken to a cutting board and strain the hot liquid into a large bowl or measuring cup. Cut each breast in half, widthwise, and use forks to pull the breast meat apart. Place in the liquid.

6. Wipe the pressure pot clean, place back in the base. Set the Cook Time for 10 minutes and press Start. Add the olive oil to the pan. When hot, add the onion and cook for 3–4 minutes or until onion begins to brown and then stir in the remaining ½ teaspoon cumin, the cayenne pepper, and the can of chopped green chilies.

7. Use tongs and add the wet pulled chicken to the pan (do not add any extra liquid other than what clings to the chicken).

8. Stir the mixture well and then pour the spicy V-8 juice over all. Cook until the mixture is heated through; close the lid, leaving the exhaust valve open (or use the glass lid) and switch the cooker to Keep Warm. Simmer 5 minutes or until you are ready to serve.

9. Serve on warm tortillas or taco shells and provide toppings as desired.

Curried Apricot Chicken

Prep Time: 15 min   **Ready in:** 45 min   **Yield:** 6–8 servings

INGREDIENTS

18" length of heavy-duty aluminum foil
3½–4-pound whole chicken
1 medium onion, quartered
2 medium cloves garlic
4 tablespoons apricot all-fruit or preserves
2 teaspoons curry powder
½ teaspoon ground coriander
½ teaspoon ground ginger
¼ teaspoon salt
1 cup chicken broth
2 tablespoons butter
2 tablespoon flour
3–4 cups cooked long grain rice

1. Place your pressure cooker on a level surface, insert the pot, and plug the unit in. Fold the aluminum foil in half lengthwise and place into the bottom of the pressure pot. This will act as a sling to help you remove the chicken after cooking.

2. Rinse chicken and pat dry with paper towels. Place the onion wedges and whole garlic cloves into the cavity of the chicken. Lower the aluminum foil into the pot and set chicken on top of it.

3. In a small bowl, combine the apricot all-fruit, curry powder, coriander, ginger, and salt to make a thin paste. Mix 1 tablespoon of the paste into the chicken broth and pour around the chicken. Use a basting brush to thoroughly coat the chicken with the remaining paste.

4. Set Cook Time to 25 minutes or select the preprogrammed Chicken button; press Start. Attach the lid and turn the pressure valve to Air Tight (closed).

5. When the Cook Time has elapsed, press Cancel to turn the machine off and release the pressure manually. Open the lid carefully. Use the aluminum foil sling to transfer the chicken from the pan to a plate. Loosely cover with foil to keep warm (use new foil if needed).

6. To make the sauce: Separate the fat from the liquid in the pan; discard fat. Remove onions and garlic from the cavity of the chicken and place in a food processor or blender with the separated liquid; process until smooth. Form a paste by stirring together the butter and flour in a small saucepan over medium heat (or you may use the Brown setting on your pressure cooker). Slowly pour in the processed liquid and bring to a gentle boil for 2–3 minutes until thick and bubbly.

7. Slice the chicken, drizzle the sauce over the slices, and serve with rice.

40-Clove Chicken

Prep Time: 15 min **Ready in:** 45 min **Yield:** 6–8 servings

INGREDIENTS

18" length of heavy-duty aluminum foil
3½–4-pound whole chicken
¼ teaspoon salt
¼ teaspoon ground black pepper
1 tablespoon olive oil
10 medium cloves garlic (each sliced into 4 pieces)
2 lemons (1 sliced, 1 halved)
1 medium onion, quartered
1 cup chicken broth

COOK'S TIP

Place the chicken under the broiler of your oven to crisp the skin. Otherwise, remove and discard the skin before serving. Serve with a crisp Caesar salad.

1. Place your pressure cooker on a level surface, insert the pot, and plug the unit in. Fold the aluminum foil in half lengthwise and set aside until it is time to place it into the bottom of the pressure pot (this will act as a sling to help you remove the chicken after cooking.)

2. Rinse chicken and pat dry. Sprinkle with the salt and pepper.

3. Set the Cook Time for 25 minutes; press Start. Add olive oil to pot.

4. When the oil is hot, place the chicken into the pan, breast down, and sear for 1–2 minutes on all sides. Remove chicken to a plate. Add the garlic and lemon slices into the pan. Sauté quickly for about 1 minute just to release the flavors. Use tongs or a spoon to remove the lemon and garlic and place into the chicken cavity, along with the onion quarters and remaining lemon halves.

5. Lower the aluminum foil into the pot and set chicken on top of it. Add chicken broth to the pot. Attach the lid and turn the pressure valve to Air Tight (closed).

6. When the Cook Time has elapsed, press Cancel to turn the machine off and release the pressure manually. Open the lid carefully. Use the aluminum foil sling to transfer the chicken from the pan to a plate. Loosely cover with foil to keep warm until ready to serve.

Chicken with Artichokes, Cream & Tomatoes

Prep Time: 10 min   **Ready in:** 40 min   **Yield:** 6 servings

INGREDIENTS

6 boneless skinless chicken breasts
1½ teaspoons salt, divided
½ teaspoon pepper, divided
2 tablespoons olive oil
1 tablespoon butter
1 small onion, finely chopped
1 cup dry white wine
1 cup chicken broth
1 tablespoon granulated chicken bouillon
14½-ounce can diced tomatoes, drained
10-ounce can artichoke hearts, drained and quartered lengthwise
1½ cups heavy cream
2 tablespoons chopped fresh basil

1. Rinse chicken and pat dry with paper towels. Season with ¾ teaspoon salt and ¼ teaspoon pepper.

2. Place your pressure cooker on a level surface, insert the pot, and plug the unit in. Set Cook Time to 12 minutes or select the preprogrammed Chicken button; press Start.

3. Add oil to pot. When oil is hot, add the chicken breasts and sauté, turning once, for 3–4 minutes or until lightly browned on both sides.

4. Add the butter, onion, wine, chicken broth, and bouillon. Bring to a boil. Attach the lid and turn the pressure valve to Air Tight (closed).

5. When the cook time has elapsed, press Cancel to turn the machine off and release the pressure manually. Open the lid carefully. Turn the chicken over and add the drained tomatoes and artichokes. Reattach lid, turn the pressure valve to Air Tight (closed), and set Cook Time for 2 minutes; press Start.

6. When Cook Time has elapsed, press Cancel to turn off the Keep Warm function and release the pressure manually. Open the lid carefully. Remove the chicken to a plate and cover with foil to keep warm. Set the Cook Time for 10 minutes and press Start.

7. Once the mixture boils, switch the pressure cooker to Keep Warm, add heavy cream and basil; simmer slowly for 5–8 minutes or until reduced to about 2 cups of liquid.

8. Taste the sauce and add the remaining salt and pepper, if desired. Return chicken to pan, cover with glass lid (or use pressure lid with valve set to Exhaust), and heat together for about 5 minutes.

Lemony Chicken

Prep Time: 10 min   **Ready in:** 25 min   **Yield:** 4–6 servings

INGREDIENTS

4 skinless, boneless chicken breast
    halves
½ teaspoon salt
¼ teaspoon pepper
¼ teaspoon thyme
2 ounces very thinly sliced prosciutto
2 tablespoons olive oil
½ cup chicken broth
¼ cup + 2 tablespoons lemon juice,
    divided
1 teaspoon cornstarch
lemon wedges, for serving

1. Rinse chicken and pat dry with paper towels. Season with salt, pepper, and thyme. Carefully wrap the chicken breasts with prosciutto. If necessary, secure with toothpick.

2. Place your pressure cooker on a level surface, insert the pot, and plug the unit in. Set Cook Time to 15 minutes or press the preprogrammed Chicken button and adjust time from there. Press Start.

3. Add the olive oil to the pot. When oil is hot, add the chicken, without overlapping, and cook, turning once, until both sides are lightly browned (3–4 minutes). Remove to a plate.

4. Add the chicken broth and 2 tablespoons of the lemon juice; scrape the bottom of the pan. Return the chicken to the pot. Attach the lid and turn the pressure valve to Air Tight (closed).

5. When the Cook Time has elapsed, release the pressure manually. Open the lid carefully. Remove chicken to a plate and cover with foil.

6. Make the sauce by selecting the Brown button or set Cook Time to 5 minutes. In a small bowl, mix the cornstarch into the remaining ¼ cup of lemon juice and pour into the boiling liquid. Simmer 2–3 minutes, until sauce slightly thickens.

7. To serve, arrange the chicken on a warm platter and pour the sauce over all. Offer lemon wedges on the side.

Turkey Breast with Gravy

Prep Time: 15 min   **Ready in:** 45 min   **Yield:** 6–8 servings

INGREDIENTS

6–7-pound turkey breast, bone-in with
  skin
1 teaspoons salt
¼ teaspoon paprika
¼ teaspoon dried thyme
1 tablespoon vegetable oil
1 medium-large white onion,
  quartered
2 stalks celery with leaves, cut into 2"
  pieces
7–8 baby carrots
2 cups chicken broth, or turkey broth
2 tablespoons butter
2 tablespoons flour

1. Rinse turkey and pat dry with paper towels. Mix the salt, paprika, and thyme together in a small bowl. Sprinkle the seasoning on the turkey skin and rub in well. Set aside.

2. Place your pressure cooker on a level surface, insert the pot, and plug the unit in. Set Cook Time to 25 minutes or press the Meat button and increase time to 25 minutes. Press Start. Add vegetable oil to the pot.

3. When oil is hot, stir in the onion, celery, and carrots. Cook for 3–4 minutes and push to the side.

4. Using tongs, place the turkey breast down into the pan. Cook 1–2 minutes, rotating as needed, until the top is lightly browned. Pour chicken broth around the turkey.

5. Reset Cook Time to 25 minutes. Attach the lid and turn the pressure valve to Air Tight (closed).

6. When the cook time has elapsed, allow the cooker to rest 10 minutes before exhausting the remaining pressure manually. Open the lid carefully. Transfer turkey breast to a carving board. Cover loosely with aluminum foil and let rest.

7. Place a small colander over a bowl or large glass measuring cup; drain the hot broth and vegetables, reserving 2 cups of broth to make the gravy. (The veggies will be overcooked but can be eaten as they are or blended into the gravy.)

8. Press the preprogrammed Brown button or set Cook Time to 10 minutes. Add the butter to the pan. When almost melted, sprinkle in the flour and stir to make a paste (about 2 minutes). Slowly add the reserved broth and bring to boil. Reduce the temperature and simmer until thick. Serve hot over sliced turkey!

Cajun Turkey Breast

Prep Time: 15 min **Ready in:** 45 min **Yield:** 6–8 servings

INGREDIENTS

6–7-pound turkey breast (bone-in, skin-on)

2 tablespoons kosher salt

1 tablespoon cayenne

1 tablespoon garlic powder

2 tablespoons sweet paprika

1 tablespoon dried oregano

1 tablespoon dried thyme

1 tablespoon freshly ground black pepper

1 tablespoon onion powder

1 tablespoon vegetable oil

1 medium-large white onion, quartered

1 medium green bell pepper, quartered, seeds and membranes removed

1 cup chicken broth, or turkey broth

COOK'S TIP

Place the turkey breast under the broiler on the low setting for 5 minutes to crisp up the skin! Otherwise, remove and discard the skin before serving. Serve with rice and top with the sauce from the pot.

1. Place your pressure cooker on a level surface, insert the pot, and plug the unit in.

2. Rinse turkey and pat dry with paper towels.

3. In a small bowl, mix the salt, cayenne, garlic powder, paprika, oregano, thyme, black pepper, and onion powder. Sprinkle this seasoning on the turkey skin and rub in well. Set aside.

4. Set Cook Time to 30 minutes or press the Meat button and increase time to 30 minutes. Press Start. Add the oil to the pan; when oil is hot, stir in the onion and bell pepper. Cook for 3–4 minutes and push to the sides of the pot.

5. Using tongs, place the turkey into the pan, breast-side down. Cook 1–2 minutes, adjusting as needed, until the breast is lightly browned. Pour broth around the turkey.

6. Check that Cook Time remains at 30 minutes or adjust as needed. Attach the lid and turn the pressure valve to Air Tight (closed).

7. When the Cook Time has elapsed, allow the cooker to rest 10 minutes before exhausting the remaining pressure manually. Open the lid carefully. Transfer turkey breast to a carving board. Cover loosely with aluminum foil and let rest.

Fish
&
Seafood

Fish & Seafood

Tips for Cooking Seafood

- Fish, shellfish, and other seafood cook quickly and deliciously in a pressure cooker. Because they cook so fast, pressure cooking is virtually the only method (other than marinating) to infuse the flavors of the broth, butter, and seasonings into the meat.
- Seafood generally has very little fat or muscle and therefore cooks very quickly. Allow 2 minutes per 1" thickness of fish or pound of shellfish. Also, if you have the option, use a low pressure setting.
- Before adding the seafood or fish to the cooker, bring the liquid to a boil first. Then add the food, quickly attach the lid, and bring up to pressure.
- Select pieces of fish with uniform size and thickness.
- For steaming, wrap fish in cheesecloth or parchment paper before pressure cooking. Place on a rack above the liquid for best results.
- Use liquid amounts as recommended by your pressure cooker's manual.
- Quick-release pressure manually, unless otherwise noted in the recipe.

Teriyaki Mahi-Mahi with Rice

Prep Time: 65 min   **Ready in:** 20 min   **Yield:** 2–4 servings

INGREDIENTS

2–4 8-ounce mahi-mahi fillets, without skin

¼ cup teriyaki sauce

2 tablespoons sesame seeds (optional)

2 tablespoons vegetable oil

2 cups uncooked long grain white rice

3½ cups chicken broth

½ teaspoon garlic salt

1 cup pineapple pieces (canned, frozen, or fresh)

COOK'S TIP
Serve this dish with fresh fruit salsa for added flavor and a pop of vibrant color!

1. Rinse the mahi-mahi and put into a zip-lock baggie with the teriyaki sauce. Place in refrigerator for 1 hour.

2. When the hour is up, remove the fish to a plate. Discard remaining teriyaki and baggie. Sprinkle the sesame seeds evenly on only one side of each fish fillet (about 1 teaspoon per fillet).

3. Place your pressure cooker on a level surface, insert the pot, and plug the unit in. Set Cook Time for 12 minutes or press the preprogrammed Rice button. Press Start.

4. Add oil to the pot. When hot, carefully place the fish fillets, seed-side down, into the pan. Sear 1–2 minutes before turning over and transferring back to a plate.

5. Add the rice to the pan along with the chicken broth and garlic salt. Stir until the rice begins to boil. Stir in the pineapple and carefully lay the fish fillets into the rice, seed-side up. Attach lid and set pressure valve to Air Tight (closed).

6. When cook time has elapsed, release pressure manually until the lid can be safely removed. Check to be sure the rice is tender. If not, remove the fish to a plate, attach lid to the pressure cooker, and cook on Keep Warm until rice is ready. Serve mahi-mahi with the rice.

Mediterranean Salmon

Prep Time: 5 min **Ready in:** 10 min **Yield:** 2–4 servings

INGREDIENTS

1-pound salmon fillet, rinsed and
  patted dry
1 halved lemon
½ teaspoon dried oregano
½ teaspoon dried parsley
1 medium tomato, seeded and
  chopped
8 small black olives, pitted and sliced
2 teaspoons capers
2 tablespoons white wine
1½ cups water
Cooked white rice (1 cup per serving),
  for serving

1. Place the salmon on a large square of aluminum foil. Squeeze the lemon over the fillet and top with oregano, parsley, tomato, olives, capers, and white wine. Pinch the foil together to form a tight packet that seals in the fish.

2. Place your pressure cooker on a level surface, insert the pot, and plug the unit in. Set Cook Time for 7 minutes or press the preprogrammed Fish button and adjust time if necessary.

3. Add the water to the bottom of the pressure cooker pot and place rack into the cooker (if available). Set the foil packet onto the rack. Attach the lid and turn the exhaust valve to the Air Tight (closed) position.

4. When cooking time has elapsed, release the pressure manually. Carefully open the lid. Carefully lift out the pouch and rack. Open foil pouch and serve fish with prepared white rice.

COOK'S TIP

This recipe can be made with just about any good-quality wild-caught fish, so experiment with your favorites!

TV TIDBIT

You may have seen this recipe made on TV. Often the fish is placed on a taller rack and the rice underneath so everything cooks together. You can absolutely do that, but increase the thickness of the fish to at least 1" to account for the increased cook time needed by the rice (increase cook time to 12 minutes).

Sweet Bourbon Salmon

Prep Time: 5 min   **Ready in:** 10 min   **Yield:** 2–4 servings

INGREDIENTS

1½ cups water

¼ cup pineapple juice

2 tablespoons soy sauce

1 tablespoon Kentucky bourbon

2 tablespoons brown sugar

¼ teaspoon cracked black pepper

⅛ teaspoon garlic powder

½ cup vegetable oil

2–4 8-ounce salmon fillets, without skin

2 tablespoons snipped fresh chives

COOK'S TIP

If you do not have a pan that will fit into your pressure cooker, make a foil pouch/bowl. If you do not have a rack, scatter a few jar lids onto the bottom of your pot!

1. Place your pressure cooker on a level surface, insert the pot, and plug the unit in. Place a meat rack (of any height) into the bottom of the cooker. Add the water.

2. Combine pineapple juice, soy sauce, bourbon, brown sugar, pepper, and garlic powder in bowl. Stir to dissolve the sugar, then add the vegetable oil.

3. Put salmon fillets into a shallow oven-safe glass dish or cake pan that fits into your pressure cooker. Pour bourbon marinade over the fish. Carefully lower the fish onto the top of the rack.

4. Attach lid and set pressure valve to the Air Tight (closed) position. Set Cook Time for 5 minutes for medium "doneness" or 7 minutes for medium-well; press Start.

5. When cook time has elapsed, release pressure manually until the lid can be safely removed. Serve salmon with a little sauce and top with fresh chives.

Mussels Marinara

Prep Time: 5 min   **Ready in:** 18 min   **Yield:** allow ½ pound of mussels per serving

INGREDIENTS

2 tablespoons olive oil
1 medium onion, diced
½ small red bell pepper, diced
¼ cup clam juice
28-ounce can crushed tomatoes
¼ cup tomato paste
1 tablespoon fresh chopped basil
(or 2 teaspoons dried)
1 tablespoon fresh chopped oregano
(or 2 teaspoons dried)
1 tablespoon fresh chopped thyme
(or 2 teaspoons dried)
1 teaspoon salt
pinch crushed red pepper
pinch sugar
2–3 pounds fresh mussels (wash,
inspect, and use only tightly closed
mussels free of cracks)
cooked linguine, for serving
hot crusty bread, for serving

1. Place your pressure cooker on a level surface, insert the pot, and plug the unit in.

2. Set Cook Time to 5 minutes or select the preprogrammed Brown button. Press Start.

3. Add oil; when oil is hot, add and sauté the onion and bell pepper for 2–3 minutes.

4. Add the rest of the ingredients, except the mussels. Attach lid and set pressure valve to Air Tight (closed). Press Cancel and set Cook Time for 10 minutes.

5. After cooking time has elapsed, quickly release the pressure and carefully remove the lid. Stir the sauce and add the mussels.

6. Replace lid, adjust valve to Air Tight (closed), and set Cook Time to 3 minutes. When cooking time has elapsed, quickly release pressure. Serve immediately with pasta and hot crusty bread.

COOK'S TIP

For a quicker version, simplify the ingredients down to 1 jar of your favorite marinara sauce, ¼ cup clam juice, and the mussels. Put everything in the pressure cooker and press Fish, or set Cook Time to 3 minutes.

Clam Sauce with Linguine

Prep Time: 7 min   **Ready in:** 13 min   **Yield:** 4 servings

INGREDIENTS

3 6½-ounce cans chopped clams
8-ounce can tomato sauce
29-ounce can diced tomatoes
2 8-ounce bottles clam juice
2 tablespoons olive oil, good quality
3 cloves garlic, minced
¾ cup coarsely chopped fresh basil
½ teaspoon crushed red pepper
1 pound uncooked linguine
grated Parmesan cheese, for serving
garlic bread, for serving

1. Open the cans of clams and drain the liquid into a measuring cup. Set aside the chopped clams. To the liquid in the measuring cup, add the tomato sauce, diced tomatoes, and clam juice.

2. Place your pressure cooker on a level surface, insert the pot, and plug the unit in. Set Cook Time to 6 minutes, or press the preprogrammed Vegetable button and adjust from there. Press Start.

3. Add olive oil to pan; when oil is hot, add garlic. Sauté about 1 minute, stirring constantly to prevent overbrowning.

4. Add basil and quickly sauté until the leaves begin to wilt. Add the crushed red pepper and stir in the tomato-water mixture.

5. Break the linguine noodles in half and add to the pot. Stir well to separate noodles, for about 1 minute. Attach lid and set the pressure valve to Air Tight (closed).

6. When cooking time has elapsed, quickly release steam. Carefully remove the lid and gently stir to separate noodles.

7. Add chopped clams, cover with glass lid (or use pressure lid with valve set to Exhaust), and simmer for 1 minute.

8. Toss together and serve with Parmesan cheese and garlic bread.

Mock Paella

Prep Time: 15 min **Ready in:** 20 min   **Yield:** 8 servings

INGREDIENTS

2 tablespoons olive oil

½ pound boneless skinless chicken
    breast, cut into small cubes

8 ounces salami, or pepperoni, cut
    into small cubes

1 medium onion, chopped

2 cloves garlic, chopped

10-ounce package yellow rice (Vigo®
    saffron yellow rice recommended)

14½-ounce can petite diced tomatoes

2 cups chicken broth

1 pound (16–20 count) shrimp, peeled
    and deveined

12 little neck clams, or mussels,
    scrubbed and bearded (optional)

3 small bay leaves

crusty bread, for serving

Tabasco®, for serving

1. Place your pressure cooker on a level
   surface, insert the pot, and plug the unit
   in. Set Cook Time to 5 minutes or select
   the preprogrammed Brown button. Press
   Start.

2. Add the olive oil; when oil is hot, add the
   chicken, salami or pepperoni, and onion.
   Cook, stirring often, for about 5 minutes.
   Add the garlic and continue cooking
   another minute.

3. Add the rice, tomatoes, and broth; stir
   well. Gently stir in the shrimp, clams or
   mussels, and bay leaves.

4. Attach the lid and set the valve to Air Tight
   (closed). Press Cancel and then select the
   preprogrammed Rice button or set Cook
   Time for 12 minutes.

5. When cooking time has elapsed, unplug
   the machine and let sit 5 minutes before
   manually releasing the remaining
   pressure. Carefully remove lid. Serve
   immediately with crusty bread and offer
   Tabasco sauce on the side.

Shrimp Scampi

Prep Time: 10 min   **Ready in:** 5 min   **Yield:** 2–4 servings

INGREDIENTS

1½ cups water

4 tablespoons butter

1 tablespoon olive oil

3 cloves garlic, coarsely chopped

2 teaspoons dried parsley flakes

½ teaspoon salt

12–24 large shrimp, peeled and
    deveined

lemon wedges

cooked linguine or rice, for serving

COOK'S TIP
If you do not have a pan that will
fit into your pressure cooker, make
a foil pouch or bowl. If you do not
have a rack, scatter a few jar lids
onto the bottom to keep your pan
above the liquid.

1. Place your pressure cooker on a level
   surface, insert the pot, and plug the unit
   in.

2. Place a meat rack (of any height) into the
   bottom of the cooker. Add the water.

3. In a microwave-safe bowl, combine the
   butter, olive oil, garlic, parsley, and salt.
   Heat in the microwave until butter is
   melted.

4. Place shrimp in a single layer into a
   shallow oven-safe glass dish or cake pan
   that fits into your pressure cooker. Pour
   butter and garlic mixture over the shrimp;
   toss to coat. Carefully lower the shrimp
   onto the top of the rack.

5. Attach lid and set pressure valve to the Air
   Tight (closed) position. Set Cook Time for
   4 minutes and press Start.

6. When cook time has elapsed, release
   pressure manually until the lid can be
   safely removed. Serve shrimp immediately
   with fresh lemon wedges, or over pasta or
   rice with a little of the garlic-butter sauce!

Shrimp Creole

Prep Time: 5 min **Ready in:** 10 min **Yield:** 2–4 servings

INGREDIENTS

½ cup corn oil
½ cup flour
1 cup chopped onions
½ cup chopped celery
¼ cup chopped green bell pepper
1 clove garlic, chopped
14½-ounce can diced tomatoes
6-ounce can tomato paste
1½ teaspoons salt
pinch red pepper flakes (add more if a
    spicier dish is desired)
¼ teaspoon black pepper
3 cups water
1½ pounds medium-sized raw
    shrimp, peeled and deveined
cooked rice, for serving
1 tablespoon chopped fresh parsley,
    for serving

1. Place your pressure cooker on a level surface, insert the pot, and plug the unit in. Set Cook Time for 5 minutes or press the preprogrammed Fish button and adjust time if necessary.

2. Add oil to pan; when oil is hot, make a roux by browning the flour in the oil over low heat. Add the onions, celery, bell pepper, and garlic and cook, stirring until soft.

3. Add diced tomatoes, tomato paste, salt, and the red and black pepper. Mix well; cook for about 2–3 minutes, then add the water.

4. Stir in the shrimp. Attach the lid and turn the exhaust valve to the Air Tight (closed) position.

5. When cooking time has elapsed, release the pressure manually. Open the lid carefully. Stir the mixture well and serve over rice. Top with chopped fresh parsley 5 minutes before serving.

Peel 'n' Eat Shrimp

Prep Time: 3 min   **Ready in:** 7 min   **Yield:** allow ⅓–½ pound per serving

INGREDIENTS
1 bottle of your favorite beer
2 pounds medium shrimp
(raw, shell-on, head-off, rinsed)
2 tablespoons Old Bay® seasoning

NEED TO FEED A CROWD?
This recipe may be increased up to 10 pounds. The rule of thumb is 1 bottle of beer per 5 pounds of shrimp and 1 tablespoon of Old Bay seasoning per pound of shrimp. If you cook more than 5 pounds, increase the time to 5 minutes.

1. Place your pressure cooker on a level surface, insert the pot, and plug the unit in. Set the Cook Time for 3 minutes or select the preprogrammed Seafood button; press Start.

2. Pour the beer into the pot; when beer is hot, add the shrimp and top with the Old Bay seasoning. Attach the lid and turn the pressure valve to Air Tight (closed).

3. When the cooking time has elapsed, place a damp paper towel loosely over the exhaust valve and release the pressure. Drain the shrimp and serve hot. Sprinkle a little more Old Bay on the shrimp, if desired.

Cajun Crawfish Boil

Prep Time: 5 min   **Ready in:** 20 min   **Yield:** 8 servings

INGREDIENTS

4 cups hot water

1 teaspoon salt

8–10 small red potatoes

8 ears of corn, halved

½ cup butter

1 pound large raw shrimp (shell on or off)

1 pound mussels, or clams

1 pound crawfish (frozen, raw, or cooked; shelled or not)

2 tablespoons crab or shrimp boil seasoning

COOK'S TIP

Base your quantities on the size of your pressure cooker! Use whatever combo of seafood you prefer, but if you add fish or lobster tails, put them in with the corn for the longer cook time!

1. Place your pressure cooker on a level surface, insert the pot, and plug the unit in. Set cooking time to 6 minutes and press Start.

2. Add the hot water, salt, and potatoes. Attach lid and set valve to Air Tight (closed).

3. When time has elapsed, switch off the Keep Warm feature and exhaust the pressure. Reset the cooking time to 6 minutes and press Start.

4. Add the corn and butter, attach lid, and set valve to Air Tight (closed).

5. When time has elapsed, switch off the Keep Warm feature and exhaust the pressure. Reset cooking time to 3 minutes and press Start.

6. Add the shrimp, mussels or clams, crawfish, and seasoning; stir well. Attach lid and set valve to Air Tight (closed).

7. When the cooking time has elapsed, switch off the Keep Warm feature and let rest 5 minutes before releasing the pressure manually.

Maine Lobsters

Prep Time: 3 min   **Ready in:** 10 min

 Yield: allow ⅓–½ pound per serving

INGREDIENTS
1 tablespoon vegetable oil
1 cup celery, cut into 2" pieces
1 cup onion, cut into quarters
3 bay leaves
1 cup water
1 tablespoon lemon juice
2–6 whole Maine lobsters
drawn butter, for serving

TV TIDBIT
On the Home Shopping Network, when Kelly opened the lid of the Elite 10-quart pressure cooker to reveal 6 jumbo lobsters, it was a thing of beauty! Fortunately for your budget, you will probably never need to cook more than 4 at a time, so the 8-quart will be perfect too!

1. Place your pressure cooker on a level surface, insert the pot, and plug the unit in. Set the Cook Time for 12 minutes or select and adjust the preprogrammed Seafood button; press Start.

2. Add the oil to the pot; when oil is hot, add the celery, onion, bay leaves, water, and lemon juice.

3. Place the lobsters into the pot in a tic-tac-toe pattern. Attach the lid and turn the pressure valve to Air Tight (closed).

4. When the cooking time has elapsed, place a damp paper towel loosely over the exhaust valve and release the pressure. Leave the lobsters in the pot until ready to serve—up to 15 minutes.

5. Serve with drawn butter.

Crab Fest

INGREDIENTS

2 cups hot water

1 teaspoon salt

2 tablespoons crab or shrimp boil seasoning

8–10 snow crab clusters

8–12 tablespoons butter, drawn, for serving

COOK'S TIP

Snow crab clusters are snow crab legs with a generous portion of the body attached. One serving consists of 2 snow crab clusters. An 8-quart cooker can easily accommodate 8–10 clusters.

1. Place your pressure cooker on a level surface, insert the pot, and plug the unit in. Set Cook Time to 5 minutes and press Start.

2. Add the hot water, salt, seasoning, and crabs. Attach lid and set valve to Air Tight (closed).

3. When time has elapsed, switch off the Keep Warm feature and exhaust the pressure. Transfer the crab legs to a platter and top with a little broth from the bottom of the pan (or serve straight from the pot to keep them warm between servings). Serve with drawn butter and lots of napkins!

Rice, Grains, Pasta & Beans

Rice, Grains, Pasta & Beans

Tips for Cooking Rice & Grains

Rinsing
- Rinsing the rice and grains is an important step that should not be skipped! Always rinse grains and rice with lukewarm water before cooking. It will help remove the starch that makes the rice sticky and clumpy as well as any dirt and debris left behind by the packaging process.

Soaking
Although rice and most grains do not require soaking, larger grains such as wheat berries and pearl barley must be soaked before cooking. It is not necessary to soak overnight—pressure soak instead! Your whole grains will cook *much* faster!

1. Pour 4 cups water and 1 cup grains into the pressure cooker. Do not add salt to the water during the soaking process as it will inhibit hydration.
2. Bring to pressure and cook 2 minutes.
3. Release pressure naturally.
4. Drain the grains and cook as directed.

Cooking
- Most electric pressure cookers will have a preset rice function or recipes specific to that model. If that's the case for your pressure cooker, be sure to follow the manufacturer's directions. Otherwise, here are some basics:
- Allow 2¼ cups water for each cup of rice along with 1 teaspoon salt and 1 tablespoon oil.
- Do **not** omit oil! It reduces foaming and clogging.
- Never fill the cooker more than halfway with rice or grains.
- Release steam using the Natural Release or Cold Water Method only.
- Remove the rice from the pan immediately to prevent overcooking or scorching.
- Wash the lid, gasket, and exhaust valve thoroughly after cooking rice and grains.

IMPORTANT
If the pressure cooker is hissing, or if any steam is escaping, it is not under full pressure. Jiggle the exhaust valve until it is silent with no steam!

Tips for Cooking Pasta

Most manufacturers make disclaimers warning against pressure cooking pasta. This is based on the fear that starches from the pasta may clog the exhaust regulator and pose a safety hazard. This is a very valid point, and extra care should be taken when cooking pasta and rice dishes. By following the tips below you *can* cook pasta . . . safely, quickly and deliciously!

- Make sure ingredients never exceed half the capacity of the cooker.
- Always add 2 tablespoons oil to the liquid to minimize the starchy foam.
- Release steam using the Natural Release or Cold Water methods only.
- Wash the lid, gasket, and exhaust valve thoroughly after cooking pasta—every time, no exceptions! If there is a metal cap covering the valve inside the lid, pop it off and wash it too! Just don't put a toothpick in the valve as it may break off.

Tips for Cooking Beans & Lentils

Most dried beans will require soaking before cooking. However, it is a much quicker process than the conventional overnight method! Just remember these two tips:

- Do not add salt during the soaking process or it will toughen the beans.
- Do not soak lentils or split peas.

Soaking

1. Pour 4 cups water and 1 cup dried beans or peas into the pressure cooker.
2. Bring to pressure and cook 5 minutes.
3. Release pressure using the cold water method.
4. Drain the beans and cook as directed.

Cooking

- Use 3 cups liquid for every 1 cup of soaked beans.
- Always add 1 tablespoon oil to the cooking water.
- Use the Natural Release method to release the steam after cooking. Do not quick-release!
- Wash the lid, gasket, and exhaust valve thoroughly before storing.

COOK'S TIP
Discarding the soaking water and replacing with fresh liquid for cooking
will cut down on the gas-producing quality of the beans.

Rice Cooking Times

Type of Rice (1 cup)	Minimum Liquid	Minimum Cook Time (Minutes)	Release Method
Arborio	2½ cups	24–25	quick or natural
Basmati	1⅔ cups	15	natural
Brown, long grain	2 cups	24–25	natural
Brown, short grain	2 cups	28–29	natural
Jasmine	1⅔ cups	15	natural
White, long grain	1⅔ cups	15	quick or natural
White, short grain	2½ cups	18	natural
Wild	4 cups	35	natural

Grain Cooking Times

Type of Grain (1 cup)	Minimum Liquid	Minimum Cook Time (Minutes)	Release Method
Barley, pearl	4½ cups	18–20	natural
Barley, whole	3 cups	20	natural
Bulgur	3 cups	8–10	natural
Corn	3½ cups	10	quick
Couscous	2 cups	3	quick
Cracked Wheat	3 cups	8–10	natural
Grits	3½ cups	10	quick
Oats, rolled	4 cups	6	natural
Oats, steel cut, Scotch, Irish, whole	4 cups	11	natural
Polenta	3½ cups	10	quick
Quinoa	2 cups	1	natural

Bean & Legume Cooking Times

Type of Bean or Legume	Soaked Cook Time (Minutes)	Unsoaked Cook Time (Minutes)	Release Method
Adzuki (aka red cow pea, red chori)	10	20	natural
Black beans	16–18	25	natural
Cannellini beans (aka white kidney)	15	35	natural
Chickpeas (aka garbonzo, kabuli)	16	35	natural
Gandules (aka pigeon peas)	16–18	25	natural
Great northern beans	15	30	natural
Kidney beans	15	35	natural
Lentils, French green	UNNECESSARY	12	quick
Lentils, green, mini brown	UNNECESSARY	10	quick
Lentils, red or yellow split	UNNECESSARY	8	quick
Lima beans, baby	6	15	natural
Lima beans, large	7	18	natural
Navy beans (aka white haricot)	17	34–40	natural
Peas, black-eyed	UNNECESSARY	12	natural
Peas, split, green, or yellow	UNNECESSARY	10	natural
Pinto beans	14	33–35	natural
Soy beans (black)	20–23	35–40	natural
Soy beans (tan)	10–12	30–35	natural

Simple Brown Rice

Prep Time: 3 min **Ready in:** 33 min **Yield:** 4–6 servings

INGREDIENTS
1½ tablespoons butter
1½ cups long grain brown rice
1 tablespoon chicken base (Better
    Than Bouillon® chicken base
    recommended)
3 cups water

COOK'S TIP
This recipe can easily be doubled, tripled, or quadrupled, depending on the size of your pressure cooker. Just be sure to increase the butter and water accordingly.

1. Place your pressure cooker on a level surface, insert the pot, and plug the unit in. Set Cook Time for 28 minutes or select the preprogrammed Brown Rice button. Press Start.

2. Add the butter to the pan. When butter is melted, add the rice. Stir until the rice is coated with the butter.

3. Mix the bouillon into the water and microwave for 3 minutes, or until the bouillon dissolves. Pour into the rice. Stir the rice well and remove spoon. Once the mixture begins to bubble, stir again.

4. Attach and lock the lid of your pressure cooker; set the pressure control to Air Tight (closed).

5. When cooking time has elapsed, release the pressure manually by opening the pressure control valve to exhaust. Once the pressure has been released, carefully open the lid and stir.

Chicken & Vegetable Risotto

 Prep Time: 20 min   **Ready in:** 1 hour 30 min   **Yield:** 6–8 servings

INGREDIENTS

3–4-pound whole fryer chicken
salt and pepper, for seasoning chicken
2 tablespoons olive oil
1 tablespoon butter
1 medium onion, coarsely chopped
5 cups chicken broth, divided
1¼ cups chopped celery
1¼ cups chopped carrots
½ pound sliced mushrooms
¼ cup chopped parsley
2 teaspoons kosher salt
1 teaspoon ground black pepper
1¾ cups Arborio rice, uncooked
¾ cup grated Parmesan cheese
additional Parmesan cheese shavings,
    for serving

COOK'S TIP
Make this quicker by using a rotisserie chicken from your local grocery or deli! Change Cook Time in Step 3 to just 10 minutes and then continue as usual.

1. Rinse chicken and pat dry with paper towels. Lightly salt and pepper chicken inside and out; set aside.

2. Place your pressure cooker on a level surface, insert the pot, and plug the unit in. Set the Cook Time to 10 minutes and press Start.

3. Add the olive oil and butter. When oil and butter are hot, add the onion and lightly brown. Add 2½ cups chicken broth and scrape the bottom of the pan with a rubber or wooden spoon. Carefully place the chicken into the pot. Attach lid and set pressure to Air Tight (closed). Press Cancel and then set Cook Time to 45 minutes.

4. When unit turns to Keep Warm, turn it off and let stand 15 minutes. Release the remaining pressure manually or by allowing it to cool naturally.

5. Using a skimmer spoon or other long-handled utensil, carefully remove the chicken and allow it to cool until you can handle it easily. Remove the bones and skin from the chicken and discard.

(Continued on next page.)

6. Using a sieve to remove any unsavory bits, strain the broth into a separate bowl or large measuring cup, and measure it. Add more chicken broth until you have a total of 4 cups. Insert the pot back into the pressure cooker and pour the 4 cups of broth into the pot.

7. Cut chicken into bite-sized pieces and return to the broth along with the remaining ingredients (except for the Parmesan cheese). Replace lid and set Cook Time for 13 minutes.

8. When cooking time has elapsed, unplug pressure cooker and let sit until no pressure remains. Carefully open the lid of your pressure cooker and gently stir in the Parmesan cheese. If the risotto is not creamy enough, add warm water or broth, ¼ cup at a time, until it reaches the perfect consistency.

9. Serve immediately, topped with shaved Parmesan cheese and a crisp green salad on the side.

Harvest Grain Pilaf

Prep Time: 11 min   **Ready in:** 33 min   **Yield:** 4–6 servings

INGREDIENTS

1½ tablespoons butter
1 cup thinly sliced leek
½ cup thinly sliced celery
2½ cups water
1½ cups chicken broth
½ cup long grain brown rice, uncooked
½ cup pearl barley, uncooked
½ cup dried cranberries, or raisins
¼ cup bulgur, uncooked
1 teaspoon sugar
½ cup almond slivers, or chopped pecans, or other chopped nuts
¼ cup fresh parsley, chopped
¼ teaspoon freshly ground black pepper

1. Place your pressure cooker on a level surface, insert the pot, and plug the unit in. Set Cook Time for 28 minutes or select the preprogrammed Brown Rice button. Press Start.

2. Add the butter to the pan. When butter is melted, add the leek and the celery. Cook 2–3 minutes. Stir in the water, broth, brown rice, and barley.

3. Attach and lock the lid of your pressure cooker; set the pressure control to Air Tight (closed).

4. When cooking time has elapsed, release the pressure manually and open the lid carefully. Stir the dried cranberries or raisins, bulgur, and sugar into the mixture. Reattach the lid and set pressure valve to Air Tight (closed). Set Cook Time for 4 minutes and press Start.

5. Meanwhile, toast almond slivers or other chopped nuts in a 350°F oven for 5 minutes.

6. When cooking time has elapsed, wait 5 minutes before releasing the pressure manually. Serve hot, topped with the toasted nuts, parsley, and pepper.

Quinoa with Lemon & Corn

Prep Time: 15 min   **Ready in:** 15 min   **Yield:** 8–10 servings

INGREDIENTS

4 ears of corn, husk and silk removed
4 cups water, divided
2 lemons, zested and juiced
1 teaspoon salt
¼ teaspoon pepper
½ tablespoon honey
¼ cup extra virgin olive oil
2 cups quinoa (white, red, or mixed)
4 scallions, whites and 1" of the
    green thinly sliced
½ cup chopped orange bell pepper
½ cup chopped fresh mint

1. Place your pressure cooker on a level surface, insert the pot, and plug the unit in. Place corn into pot and add 1 cup of water. Attach and lock the lid of your pressure cooker and set the pressure control to Air Tight (closed). Set Cook Time for 3 minutes; press Start.

2. When cooking time has elapsed, release the pressure manually. Open the lid carefully and use tongs to transfer corn to a cutting board. When cool enough to handle, cut kernels off cobs with heavy knife or mandolin. Set aside.

3. Meanwhile, in a large bowl, whisk together the lemon zest and juice, salt, pepper, and honey. Continue whisking while slowly drizzling in the olive oil.

4. Remove pot from pressure cooker. Wash, dry, and return the pot to the cooker.

5. Place quinoa into a fine-meshed sieve and wash three times, or until water runs clear. Place quinoa into pressure pot and stir in the remaining 3 cups of water.

6. Attach and lock the lid of your pressure cooker and set the pressure control to Air Tight (closed). Set Cook Time for 1 minute; press Start. When cooking time has elapsed, let pressure release naturally.

7. Carefully open the lid of your pressure cooker and transfer the qunioa into the bowl containing your lemon mixture; mix well. Gently stir in the corn kernels, scallions, bell pepper, and mint. Serve immediately.

Quinoa with Toasted Pine Nuts

Prep Time: 15 min   **Ready in:** 15 min   **Yield:** 8–10 servings

INGREDIENTS

2 cups quinoa (white, red, or mixed)

2 teaspoons olive oil

6 medium scallions

1 tablespoon minced garlic

2½ cups chicken broth

½ cup pine nuts

½ cup fresh basil leaves, sliced into ribbons

½ teaspoon salt

½ teaspoon freshly ground black pepper

1. Place quinoa into a fine-meshed sieve and wash three times, or until water runs clear; set aside.

2. Prepare scallions by slicing the white and light green from four scallions into thin rings. With the remaining two scallions, cut the light green parts lengthwise into long, thin pieces (discard the white parts from these two scallions).

3. Place your pressure cooker on a level surface, insert the pot, and plug the unit in. Set Cook Time to 1 minute, press Start. Add olive oil to the pot; when oil is hot, add the sliced scallion rings; stir quickly. Add the garlic and sauté just 1 minute.

4. Stir in the quinoa and the chicken broth. Attach and lock the lid of your pressure cooker and set the pressure control to Air Tight (closed).

5. When cooking time has elapsed, let pressure release naturally.

6. Meanwhile, place the pine nuts in a hot pan on the stove and cook 3 minutes or until beginning to brown. You may also brown the nuts in the oven if you prefer.

7. Carefully open the lid of your pressure cooker. Gently stir in the basil, salt, and pepper.

8. Serve in bowls, topped with remaining scallion strips and toasted pine nuts.

Easy Macaroni & Cheese

Prep Time: 5 min   **Ready in:** 25 min   **Yield:** 8–10 servings

INGREDIENTS

3 tablespoons butter

1 tablespoon olive oil

1 pound Velveeta cheese, cut into
   large cubes

½ teaspoon dry mustard

½ teaspoon salt

½ teaspoon paprika

4 cups hot water

1 pound large elbow macaroni

½ cup milk, optional

2 cups shredded Colby Jack or mild
   cheddar cheese

TV TIDBIT

Mac 'n' cheese has quickly
become one of the most requested
demo recipes ever! Although I
don't recommend cooking more
than 2 pounds of pasta at one
time, you may want to add ¼ cup
chopped jalapeño peppers and
1 small jar of chopped pimiento
peppers like we do on TV. It really
peps up the color and flavor!

1. Place your pressure cooker on a level
   surface, insert the pressure pot, and
   plug the unit in. Set the Cook Time to 10
   minutes or select the preprogrammed Rice
   button and adjust the time to 10 minutes.

2. Add the butter and oil to the pot. When
   butter starts to melt, add the Velveeta
   cheese cubes and stir well as they begin to
   melt. Don't let the cheese brown!

3. Stir in the seasonings, water, and
   macaroni. Attach lid and set exhaust valve
   to Air Tight (closed). Press Cancel to stop
   the timer and then select Rice; press Start.

4. When cooking time has elapsed, press
   Cancel and wait 2–3 minutes before
   releasing the pressure manually.

5. Carefully open the lid and stir gently but
   well. Add milk to make it creamier, if
   desired. Add the shredded cheese to the
   top. Cover with a glass lid or the pressure
   lid, leaving the valve on Exhaust. Serve
   once the cheese has melted.

Lasagna

Prep Time: 10 min   **Ready in:** 30 min   **Yield:** 4–6 servings

INGREDIENTS

1 tablespoon olive oil

1½ pounds lean ground beef

1 medium onion, finely chopped

1 medium green bell pepper, seeds and membrane removed, finely chopped

26-ounce jar spaghetti sauce

1½ cups crushed tomatoes, divided

32 ounces ricotta cheese, part skim

1 cup grated Parmesan cheese

3 cups shredded mozzarella cheese, divided

1 large egg

2 teaspoons garlic salt

2 teaspoons dried basil

2 teaspoons dried oregano

1 tablespoon dried parsley

8-ounce package no-cook lasagna noodles

1. Place your pressure cooker on a level surface, insert the pot, and plug the unit in. Select the preprogrammed Meat button or set the Cook Time to 12 minutes; press Start.

2. Add the oil to the pan; when oil is hot, add ground beef. Cook 5 minutes, turning and stirring often. Add the onion and bell pepper and cook another minute. Add the spaghetti sauce and 1 cup of the crushed tomatoes. Stir well. Attach and close lid, and set exhaust valve to Air Tight (closed).

3. Meanwhile, in a medium mixing bowl, combine the ricotta cheese, Parmesan cheese, 1½ cups shredded mozzarella, egg, garlic salt, and herbs.

4. When cooking time has elapsed, manually exhaust the pressure and carefully open the lid. Very carefully remove the pot and pour the hot meat sauce into a bowl or large measuring cup. Return pot to pressure cooker.

5. Fill the bottom of the cooker with the remaining ½ cup crushed tomatoes and spread as evenly as you can. Layer the noodles on top (I can usually only fit 2 whole noodles in the bottom, and then I break a noodle into 4 strips to fill in the gaps).

6. Cover the noodles with a quarter of the cheese mixture. Cover the cheese with 2 ladles' worth of meat sauce, then another layer of noodles. Repeat until all noodles have been used. The topmost layer should be noodles topped with sauce.

7. Lock the lid and set pressure valve to Air Tight (closed). When cooking time has elapsed, quick-release pressure and sprinkle with remaining 1½ cups mozzarella cheese. Cover and allow to rest for 10 minutes before serving.

Tortellini Alfredo

Prep Time: 7 min   **Ready in:** 30 min   **Yield:** 4–6 servings

INGREDIENTS

3 tablespoons olive oil

½ pound sliced mushrooms

½-pound ham steak, cut into small cubes

1 teaspoon garlic salt

¼ teaspoon ground black pepper

1 cup hot water

12-ounce package of dried three-cheese tortellini (Barilla® recommended)

2 cups frozen peas

2 15-ounce jars of Alfredo sauce, warmed

warm milk, to adjust consistency as desired

1–2 ounces finely shredded Parmesan cheese, for serving

1. Place your pressure cooker on a level surface, insert the pot, and plug the unit in. Select the preprogrammed Rice button or set the Cook Time to 12 minutes; press Start.

2. Add the oil to the pan; when oil is hot, add mushrooms. Cook quickly for 2–3 minutes, then add the ham, garlic salt, and pepper. Continue cooking to warm the ham.

3. Add the water, tortellini, peas, and Alfredo sauce; stir well. Attach and close lid and set exhaust valve to Air Tight (closed). Press Cancel to stop the timer and then select Rice; press Start.

4. When cooking time has elapsed, press Cancel and wait 2 minutes before releasing the pressure manually. Open the lid carefully and stir gently. If the mixture is too thick, stir in a little warm milk until you achieve your desired consistency. Serve hot with shredded Parmesan cheese.

COOK'S TIP

To make this a protein-complete meal, try it with shrimp or chicken! Just add 1 pound medium shrimp (peeled and deveined) or 1 pound chicken breast (cut into bite-sized cubes) at the end of step 2, then continue as usual!

Cheesy Penne with Chicken

Prep Time: 10 min   **Ready in:** 25 min   **Yield:** 8–10 servings

INGREDIENTS

4 slices bacon or ham
2 tablespoons vegetable oil
½ cup onion, finely chopped
½ pound sliced mushrooms
½ cup rotisserie or baked chicken,
　　chopped or shredded into
　　bite-sized pieces
1 teaspoon garlic salt
½ teaspoon coarse ground black
　　pepper
2 cups water
2 cups chicken broth
1 pound penne pasta
8 ounces cream cheese
8 ounces shredded Monterey Jack,
　　or sharp cheddar cheese
¼ cup milk

1. Place your pressure cooker on a level surface, insert the pot, and plug the unit in. Select the preprogrammed Rice button or set the Cook Time to 12 minutes; press Start.

2. Add bacon or ham slices to pot and cook until brown and crispy. Remove and drain on paper towel.

3. Wash, dry, and replace the pot. Add oil; when oil is hot, add onion and mushrooms. Cook quickly for 2–3 minutes and then add the chicken, garlic salt, and pepper. Add water, broth, and pasta. Stir well.

4. Attach and close lid and set exhaust valve to Air Tight (closed). Press Cancel to stop the timer and then select Rice; press Start.

5. When cooking time has elapsed, press Cancel and wait 2 minutes before manually releasing the pressure. Carefully open the lid and stir well, adding the cheeses and, if necessary, the milk until creamy and well blended.

6. Attach the lid, but keep the exhaust valve open. Keep the pressure cooker on the Keep Warm setting. Check the pasta every minute, stirring gently, until it has reached desired tenderness.

Black Beans

Prep Time: 15 min **Ready in:** 90 min **Yield:** 8–10 servings

INGREDIENTS

1 pound black beans, rinsed and
   picked clean
cold water
1 green bell pepper
2 tablespoons olive oil
1 large yellow onion, diced
2 cloves garlic, minced
6 cups water
1 large smoked ham hock
2 bay leaves
½ teaspoon salt
½ teaspoon cumin
½ teaspoon paprika
cooked white rice, for serving (optional)
additional diced onion, for serving
   (optional)

1. Place your pressure cooker on a level surface, insert the pot, and plug the unit in. Add black beans to the pot and cover by 2 inches with cold water (about 5 cups for an 8-quart pressure cooker).

2. Cut the green bell pepper in half. Remove seeds and membrane. Dice only one half of the bell pepper and set aside. Add the other intact half to the beans.

3. Attach and lock the lid; set the pressure control to Air Tight (closed). Set Cook Time for 5 minutes; press Start. When cooking time has elapsed, press Cancel to turn off the Keep Warm setting and let pressure release naturally.

4. Carefully open the lid. Remove and discard green pepper half. Carefully remove the pot and pour the beans through a colander to drain. Rinse the beans well, drain again, and set aside.

5. Wash, dry, and replace the pressure pot into the cooker base. Set Cook Time for 40 minutes or press the preprogrammed Bean button. Add oil; when oil is hot, add the onion, diced bell pepper, and garlic. Reduce heat to medium and sauté for 3–4 minutes until the onion is soft but not brown.

6. Add 6 cups water, the ham hock, bay leaves, salt, cumin, and paprika. Add the beans and bring to a boil. Attach the lid and set the regulator to Air Tight (closed).

7. When cooking time has elapsed, let pressure release naturally and remove the lid. Discard the ham hock and bay leaves. Using a slotted spoon, remove 1 cup of beans to a bowl and mash them. Return the mashed beans to the pot and stir well. Cook uncovered over Keep Warm another 15 minutes. Serve alone or over cooked white rice; top with additional diced onion.

Cowboy Beans

Prep Time: 10 min   **Ready in:** 25 min   **Yield:** 8–10 servings

INGREDIENTS

1 pound lean ground beef

2 tablespoons vegetable oil

1 cup onion, coarsely chopped

1 cup green bell pepper, coarsely chopped

1 cup brown sugar

6-ounce can tomato paste

2 teaspoons mustard powder

1 teaspoon chili powder

2 teaspoon Worcestershire sauce

2 cups water

27-ounce can light red kidney beans, drained

27-ounce can dark red kidney beans, drained

2 16-ounce cans chili beans, undrained

COOK'S TIP

This can be made easily from dried beans by following the time charts on page 179 to soak and cook them before adding to this recipe!

COOK'S TIP

For a "baked bean" flavor, finish the dish off by transferring to a baking dish, sprinkling lightly with brown sugar, and cooking in a 350°F oven 15–20 minutes.

1. Place your pressure cooker on a level surface, insert the pot, and plug the unit in. Set the Cook Time to 9 minutes and press Start.

2. Add ground beef and cook until browned, stirring often. Drain and set aside.

3. Add oil, onion, and bell pepper and cook for about 2 minutes or until onion is starting to soften but is not yet browned.

4. Add the brown sugar, tomato paste, mustard powder, chili powder, Worcestershire sauce, and water. Gently stir until the mixture is bubbly and well mixed.

5. Stir in the ground beef and all the beans. Attach and close lid and set exhaust valve to Air Tight (closed).

6. When cooking time has elapsed, unplug pressure cooker and let the pressure release naturally. Serve warm.

Quick Red Beans & Rice

Prep Time: 10 min   **Ready in:** 20 min   **Yield:** 6–8 servings

INGREDIENTS

2 tablespoons olive oil

3 tablespoons butter

1 cup coarsely chopped onion

1 cup coarsely chopped green bell pepper

½ pound kielbasa, sliced thin (optional)

27-ounce can light red kidney beans, drained

2 cups converted rice (uncooked)

1 tablespoon creole seasoning, to taste

4¾ cups hot water

COOK'S TIP
This can be made easily from dried beans by following the time charts on page 179 to soak and cook them before adding to this recipe!

1. Place your pressure cooker on a level surface, insert the pot, and plug the unit in. Set the Cook Time to 9 minutes and press Start.

2. Add oil, butter, onion, and bell pepper. If desired, add sliced kielbasa.

3. Cook for about 2 minutes, or until onion is starting to soften but is not yet browned.

4. Add the beans, rice, and seasoning and stir well. Add the water and stir again. Attach and close lid and set exhaust valve to Air Tight (closed).

5. When cooking time has elapsed, unplug pressure cooker and let sit 5 minutes and then manually release the pressure (or you may allow pressure to release naturally).

Chickpeas & Spinach

Prep Time: 10 min   **Ready in:** 75 min   **Yield:** 8–10 servings

INGREDIENTS

2 tablespoons olive oil

1 medium yellow onion, finely chopped

1 green bell pepper, seeds and membrane removed, finely chopped

2 cups chicken or vegetable broth

1 cup water

1 teaspoon paprika

¼ teaspoon dried minced garlic

½ teaspoon salt

1 pound dried chickpeas, rinsed and picked clean

2 cups frozen spinach, thawed and squeezed dry

1 fire-roasted red bell pepper, skinned and cut into very thin strips

1. Place your pressure cooker on a level surface, insert the pot, and plug the unit in. Set Cook Time for 45 minutes or press the preprogrammed Bean button.

2. Add oil; when oil is hot, add the onion and green bell pepper. Cook about 2–3 minutes and then stir in the broth, water, paprika, garlic, salt, and chickpeas. Attach the lid and set the regulator to Air Tight (closed).

3. When cooking time has elapsed, let pressure release naturally and remove the lid. Stir in the thawed spinach and fire-roasted pepper.

4. Reset Cook Time for 12 minutes or press the Rice button. Reattach lid and set exhaust valve to Air Tight (closed).

5. When cook time has elapsed, let sit 10 minutes before releasing the pressure. Serve in a bowl or drain and use as a topping on tortilla chips or pita wedges.

Desserts

Desserts

Tips for Cooking Desserts & Sweets

- Desserts that use eggs and/or are cooked over a water bath—such as cheesecakes, custards, lemon curds, and puddings—turn out quite delicious in a pressure cooker!
- The timing is tricky with cheesecakes and other thick batters. Use room temperature ingredients to speed the cooking process and do not overfill the pan.
- If your cooker did not come with baking dishes, be sure to select a dish that is oven-safe and will fit into your pressure cooker with at least 1" to spare around the edge.
- Always seal the dish tightly with foil to keep liquid from seeping into the dessert.
- For easy insertion and removal, use a sling made of aluminum foil or a steamer basket under the baking dish.
- Never place the dish directly onto the bottom of the cooker. Use a steamer basket or rack or scatter jar lids to keep the dish raised.
- When adapting non-pressure cooker recipes, use the minimum liquid required as there will be no evaporation or boil-off in the pressure cooker.

Stuffed Apples

Prep Time: 10 min   **Ready in:** 7 min   **Yield:** 2–4 servings

INGREDIENTS

2–4 large apples (gala or fuji recommended, but any firm red apple will work)
½ cup dried cherries, dried cranberries, or raisins
¼ cup brown sugar
¼ cup chopped pecans
½ teaspoon ground cinnamon
1 tablespoon butter
1 cup apple juice
vanilla ice cream, for serving

1. Prepare the apples by using a melon baller to hollow out the inside of the apple. The opening should be big enough to hold a little stuffing. Avoid making the walls too thin, or they'll become mushy during the cooking process.

2. Make the stuffing by tossing together the dried fruit, brown sugar, pecans, and cinnamon. Place the stuffing inside the hollowed-out apples; set aside.

3. Place your pressure cooker on a level surface, insert the pot, and plug the unit in. Set Cook Time for 3 minutes or press the Vegetable/Fish button. Press Start.

4. Add the butter to the pot. When butter is melted, add the apple juice and bring to a simmer.

5. Place the apples into the pot. Attach the lid and turn the pressure valve to Air Tight (closed).

6. When cooking time has elapsed, immediately release the pressure manually. Open the lid and use tongs to carefully remove the apples. Serve with vanilla ice cream.

Poached Pears

Prep Time: 10 min   **Ready in:** 7 min   **Yield:** 2–6 servings

INGREDIENTS

2–6 pears
3 tablespoons butter
1 cup port wine
2 cinnamon sticks
**optional toppings: chocolate sauce,
    whipped cream, ice cream, and/or
    chopped nuts**

COOK'S TIP
The hot tartness of the pears
goes perfect with the coolness of
whipped cream or ice cream. Add a
little chocolate sauce, and you have
a delicious, easy dessert!

1. For each pear, peel all but the very bottom and very top.

2. Place your pressure cooker on a level surface, insert the pot, and plug the unit in. Set Cook Time for 7 minutes or press the Vegetable/Fish button and adjust. Press Start

3. Add the butter to the pot. When butter is melted, add the port wine and cinnamon sticks and bring to a simmer.

4. Place the pears into the pot. Attach the lid and turn the pressure valve to Air Tight (closed).

5. When cooking time has elapsed, wait 5 minutes and release the remaining pressure manually. Open the lid and use tongs to serve the pears.

6. If desired, serve pears with a drizzle of chocolate sauce, a dollop of whipped cream, or a scoop of ice cream. Sprinkle chopped nuts, if desired.

Pumpkin Cheesecake

Prep Time: 15 min **Ready in:** 4 hours **Yield:** 8 servings

INGREDIENTS
butter for greasing pan
1 cup cinnamon graham cracker crumbs
¼ cup granulated sugar
4 tablespoons butter, melted
12 ounces cream cheese, softened
1 teaspoon vanilla
1 tablespoon butter, room temperature
¾ cup brown sugar, firmly packed
¾ cup pureed pumpkin
2 tablespoons cornstarch
1 teaspoon cinnamon
¾ teaspoon nutmeg
3 large eggs
2 cups hot water

1. Generously butter bottom and sides of a 6" or 8" springform pan (or the size that will fit inside your pressure cooker). Sprinkle graham cracker crumbs and sugar evenly on bottom of pan; drizzle the melted butter over all. Mix lightly with fork and then press the mixture onto the bottom of the pan. Set aside.

2. In large mixing bowl, mix together cream cheese, vanilla, and butter.

3. Add brown sugar, pumpkin, cornstarch, cinnamon, and nutmeg. Continue mixing. Mix in 1 egg at a time until smooth.

4. Pour into pan, filling up to ½" from the lip. If using a 6" pan, do not fill the pan more than ⅔ full; save the batter for another use or discard.

5. Cover top with waxed paper and then completely cover entire pan with aluminum foil, crimping top and bottom edges to seal out moisture.

6. Place your pressure cooker on a level surface, insert the pot, and plug the unit in. Place rack or riser in bottom of 8-quart pressure cooker. Add the hot water to the pot, then lower cake pan to rest on top of the rack. Attach the lid and turn the pressure valve to Air Tight (closed).

7. Set Cook Time for 50 minutes for a 6" cake or 40 minutes for an 8" cake. Press Start.

8. When cooking time has elapsed, press Cancel and wait 30 minutes.

9. Remove cheesecake from pan, remove the foil (be careful not to get liquid onto the cheese cake), and refrigerate at least 3 hours.

10. Open and expand the springform pan, and remove the exterior ring from the cheesecake. Cover with Spiced Whipped Topping. Slice and enjoy!

For spiced whipped topping:
1 pint heavy whipping cream
½ cup powdered sugar
¼ teaspoon nutmeg
½ teaspoon cinnamon + extra for garnish
chocolate curls or shavings, for garnish

1. Use the highest speed of your electric hand mixer to whisk together the heavy whipping cream, powdered sugar, nutmeg, and ½ teaspoon cinnamon.

2. When thick, spread over the top of cooled cheesecake. Sprinkle the remaining cinnamon on top and garnish with chocolate curls or shavings. Return cheesecake to refrigerator until ready to serve.

Lemon Cheesecake

Prep Time: 15 min   **Ready in:** 4 hours   **Yield:** 8 servings

INGREDIENTS

butter, for greasing pan
6 graham crackers
1 tablespoon granulated sugar
4 tablespoons melted butter
16 ounces cream cheese, room
    temperature (do not use reduced
    fat varieties)
1½ cups confectioners' sugar
1 teaspoon lemon zest
3 tablespoons cornstarch
2 eggs, at room temperature
¼ teaspoon almond extract (optional)
4 tablespoons fresh lemon juice
1½ cups water
optional toppings: whipped cream,
    fresh fruit, glaze, or cherry or
    blueberry pie filling

COOK'S TIP
Store any leftovers in an airtight
container in the refrigerator or
freeze for up to 6 months.

1. Generously butter bottom and sides of a springform pan (or the size that will fit into your pressure cooker). Sprinkle graham cracker crumbs and sugar evenly on bottom of pan; drizzle the melted butter over all. Mix lightly with fork and then press the mixture onto the bottom of the pan. Set aside.

2. In large mixing bowl, mix together cream cheese, confectioners' sugar, lemon zest, and cornstarch. Beat in eggs, one at a time; then add almond extract and slowly drizzle in the lemon juice.

3. Pour batter into prepared springform pan. Cover top with waxed paper and then completely cover entire pan with aluminum foil, crimping top and bottom edges to seal out moisture.

4. Place your pressure cooker on a level surface, insert the pot, and plug in the unit. Set Cook Time to 45 minutes and press Start. Pour the water into the cooker and center the steaming rack inside. Place the covered cheesecake on top of the rack. Attach the lid and turn the pressure valve to Air Tight (closed).

5. When the cooking time has elapsed, turn the cooker off and let the cake remain inside for 10 minutes or until no pressure remains. Carefully open the lid, remove the cake to a cooling rack, and gently remove the foil.

6. Serve warm (within the next 20 minutes), at room temperature (after about 45 minutes), or chilled (cover with plastic wrap and place in the refrigerator for at least 4 hours).

7. To serve, gently run a thin knife around the edge of the cake before unlatching and removing the sides of the springform pan. If desired, top with whipped cream, fresh fruit, glaze, or cherry or blueberry pie filling.

Coconut Rice Pudding

Prep Time: 10 min   **Ready in:** 15 min   **Yield:** 6 servings

INGREDIENTS

3 cups jasmine rice

3 tablespoons butter

3½ cups water

¼ cup sugar

3 cans coconut milk

2 7-ounce bags Sun Maid® tropical trio
    dried fruit

2 cups coconut flakes

½ cup half-and-half

COOK'S TIP
Refrigerate leftovers and serve cold
or reheat in the microwave on the
medium setting.

1. Place your pressure cooker on a level surface, insert the pot, and plug the unit in. Set Cook Time for 12 minutes or press the Rice button. Press Start

2. To the pot, add the rice, butter, water, sugar, and coconut milk. Stir well. Set aside a little of the dried fruit for garnish and stir the rest into the rice mixture. Attach the lid and turn the pressure valve to Air Tight (closed).

3. Meanwhile, toast the coconut flakes in the oven for 4–5 minutes at 350°F.

4. When cooking time has elapsed, wait 5 minutes and release the remaining pressure manually.

5. Open the lid and carefully stir the rice. Stir in the half-and-half if needed to thicken.

6. Attach lid to the pressure cooker (set to Exhaust) or use glass lid. Let rest 5 minutes.

7. Stir well and serve hot with toasted coconut flakes.

Banana Nut Rice Pudding

Prep Time: 10 min   **Ready in:** 15 min   **Yield:** 8 servings

INGREDIENTS

- 2 cups long grain white rice
- 3 tablespoons butter
- ¼ cup light, amber agave syrup + extra for serving
- 3 cups water
- 3 cups milk
- 1 teaspoon cinnamon
- ¼ teaspoon nutmeg
- 1 cup pecan halves
- ½ teaspoon imitation banana flavoring (optional)
- ½ cup half-and-half
- 2 fresh ripe bananas

COOK'S TIP
Refrigerate leftovers and serve cold, or reheat in the microwave on medium-power setting. Pudding may need to be thinned with a little half-and-half if reheating.

1. Place your pressure cooker on a level surface, insert the pot, and plug the unit in. Set Cook Time for 8 minutes. Press Start.

2. Add the rice, butter, agave syrup, water, milk, cinnamon, and nutmeg to the pot and stir well. Attach the lid and turn the pressure valve to Air Tight (closed).

3. Meanwhile, toast the pecan halves in the oven for 5–6 minutes at 350°F. Cool and chop coarsely.

4. When cooking time has elapsed, wait 5 minutes and release the remaining pressure manually. Open the lid and carefully stir the rice. Stir in the banana flavoring (if desired) and half-and-half.

5. Attach lid to the pressure cooker, (set to Exhaust) or use glass lid. Let rest 5 minutes. While you wait, slice the fresh bananas.

6. When resting time is finished, stir the pudding well. Serve hot with fresh banana slices, chopped pecans, and a drizzle of agave.

Hawaiian Bread Pudding

Prep Time: 20 min   **Ready in:** 30 min   **Yield:** 8 servings

INGREDIENTS
butter or shortening, for greasing dish
8 Hawaiian sweet rolls
2¼ cups milk
1 tablespoon butter
½ cup brown sugar
¼ teaspoon salt
½ teaspoon cinnamon
½ teaspoon vanilla extract
¼ teaspoon rum extract (optional)
2 eggs, beaten
¼ cup dried mango
¼ cup dried cranberries
¼ cup dried pineapple
4 cups hot water
optional toppings: whipped cream,
     caramel sauce, toasted coconut flakes

COOK'S TIP
If you don't have a rack, you can make a sling! Take a 2-foot-long piece of foil and fold it into thirds. Use the sling to help lower and raise the dish in and out of the pressure pan.

1. Place pressure cooker onto a level surface, insert the pot, and plug in the unit. With butter or shortening, grease the inside of a 2-quart oven-safe bowl or dish that will fit inside the pressure cooker pot.

2. Prepare the bread by first cutting the browned top off of each roll and setting aside. Cut the bottom portion of the rolls into quarters and place inside prepared dish.

3. Place the milk into a microwave-safe dish and heat on high for 3 minutes. To the milk, add the butter, brown sugar, salt, cinnamon, and both extracts and stir completely.

4. Stir in the beaten eggs and pour three-fourths of the mixture over the bread cubes. Sprinkle three-fourths of the dried fruit on top of the mixture.

5. Arrange the tops of the rolls evenly over the contents of the dish. Pour the remaining milk mixture over everything and top with the remaining fruit. Cover the dish tightly with aluminum foil.

6. Place a low- to mid-height rack into the cooker (or make a sling: see Cook's Tip on previous page) and pour water into the bottom of the pot. Carefully lower the sealed bread pudding onto the rack. (Make sure the water doesn't seep into the pudding.) Attach the lid and turn the pressure valve to Air Tight (closed). Set Cook Time to 25 minutes and press Start.

7. When the cooking time has elapsed, turn the cooker off and let the cake remain inside for 10 minutes or until no pressure remains. Carefully open the lid and remove the cake to a rack. Gently remove the foil.

8. Serve the pudding immediately with whipped cream, caramel sauce, toasted coconut flakes, or all by itself! Store leftovers in the refrigerator.

Pineapple Upside-Down Cake

Prep Time: 10 min   **Ready in:** 1 hour   **Yield:** 8 servings

INGREDIENTS

1 pineapple cake mix
3 tablespoons butter
¼ cup light brown sugar
20-ounce can pineapple chunks, drained
10-ounce jar maraschino cherries, drained

1. Prepare the cake batter according to package directions.

2. Place pressure cooker on a level surface, insert the pot, and plug in the unit. Set Cook Time for 40 minutes or select the Cake setting. Press Start.

3. Add the butter to the pot. When butter is melted, add the brown sugar, pineapple chunks, and cherries. Stir until blended.

4. Pour the prepared cake batter over the fruit.

5. When cooking time has elapsed, let pressure release naturally. Open the lid and allow to cool for 5–10 minutes before flipping onto a platter.

Chocolate Cherry Gooey Cake

Prep Time: 15 min   **Ready in:** 2 hours   **Yield:** 8 servings

INGREDIENTS

21-ounce can cherry pie filling, divided
15¼-ounce triple chocolate fudge cake mix
¼ cup vegetable oil
3 large eggs
3 cups water, divided

1. Scoop half of the cherry pie filling into the bottom of a stainless steel mixing bowl; set aside.

2. In a large mixing bowl, combine the cake mix, oil, eggs, and 1 cup water. Mix until smooth. Gently mix in the remaining pie filling until completely incorporated.

3. Pour the batter over the cherries in the mixing bowl.

4. Place your pressure cooker on a level surface, insert the pot, and plug in the unit. Set Cook Time to 90 minutes and press Start. Pour 2 cups water into the cooker and center the steaming rack inside.

5. Completely cover the top of the mixing bowl with aluminum foil, pinching around the rim to keep moisture out. Place the covered bowl into the cooker and set on the rack. (If your mixing bowl has silicone on the bottom, you can skip the rack.)

6. Attach the lid and turn the pressure valve to Air Tight (closed).

7. When the cooking time has elapsed, turn the cooker off and let the cake remain inside for 10 minutes or until no pressure remains. Carefully open the lid, remove the mixing bowl to a cooling rack, and gently remove the foil.

8. Serve warm (within the next 20 minutes), at room temperature (after about 45 minutes), or chilled (cover with plastic wrap and place in the refrigerator for at least 4 hours).

9. To serve, gently run a thin knife around the edge of the cake to release from the edges of the bowl. Place a plate over the top and flip the cake onto the plate.

Cinnamon Apple Cake

Prep Time: 15 min **Ready in:** 45 min **Yield:** 8 servings

INGREDIENTS

15¼-ounce yellow cake mix

1 cup water

⅓ cup vegetable oil

3 large eggs

2 apples, one peeled and shredded (about 1 cup) and the other cored and sliced on a mandolin

1½ teaspoons cinnamon, divided

3 tablespoons brown sugar, divided

3 tablespoons butter

1. In a large mixing bowl, combine the cake mix, water, oil, and eggs. Mix until smooth. Set aside.

2. In a small bowl, combine the shredded apple with 1 teaspoon cinnamon and 2 tablespoons brown sugar until completely mixed. Set aside.

3. Place your pressure cooker on a level surface, insert the pot, and plug in the unit. Set Cook Time to 30 minutes or select the Desserts button and press Start.

4. Add the butter to the pot. When hot, add the sliced apples, ½ teaspoon cinnamon, and 1 tablespoon brown sugar. Stir well to coat and then spread the slices in a single layer on the bottom of the pot.

5. Pour half of the cake batter over the apples. Layer on the shredded apple mixture; try to arrange the apples evenly and use any juice that may have formed. Top with the remaining cake batter. Attach the lid and turn the pressure valve to Air Tight (closed).

6. When the cooking time has elapsed, turn the cooker off and let the cake remain inside for 10 minutes or until no pressure remains. Carefully open the lid and remove the pot.

7. To serve, gently run a thin knife around the edge of the cooked cake to loosen it from the sides of the pot. Place plate over the top and invert the cake onto the plate.

Blueberry Pear Cobbler

Prep Time: 15 min   **Ready in:** 40 min   **Yield:** 8 servings

INGREDIENTS

1½ cups self-rising flour
1½ cups sugar
1 cup milk
2 pears, peeled, cored, and sliced
1 teaspoon cinnamon
2 tablespoons brown sugar
4 tablespoons butter
21-ounce can blueberry pie filling
homemade whipped cream, for
    serving

COOK'S TIP
This is equally delicious using
peaches and/or blackberries!

1. In a large mixing bowl, combine the flour, sugar, and milk. Mix until smooth. Set batter aside.

2. In a separate bowl, toss together the pears, cinnamon, and the brown sugar until completely mixed. Set aside.

3. Place your pressure cooker on a level surface, insert the pot, and plug in the unit. Set Cook Time to 18 minutes or select the Desserts button and press Start.

4. Add the butter to the pan. When hot, pour in the batter. Immediately top with the can of blueberry pie filling; spread as evenly as you can.

5. Place the sliced pears in a decorative pattern across the top of the blueberry filling. Attach the lid and turn the pressure valve to Air Tight (closed).

6. When the cooking time has elapsed, turn the cooker off and let the cake remain inside for 10 minutes or until no pressure remains. Carefully open the lid.

7. Serve with homemade whipped cream!

Conversion Charts

METRIC AND IMPERIAL CONVERSIONS

(These conversions are rounded for convenience)

Ingredient	Cups/Tablespoons/Teaspoons	Ounces	Grams/Milliliters
Butter	1 cup = 16 tablespoons = 2 sticks	8 ounces	230 grams
Cheese, shredded	1 cup	4 ounces	110 grams
Cream cheese	1 tablespoon	0.5 ounce	14.5 grams
Cornstarch	1 tablespoon	0.3 ounce	8 grams
Flour, all-purpose	1 cup/1 tablespoon	4.5 ounces/0.3 ounce	125 grams/8 grams
Flour, whole wheat	1 cup	4 ounces	120 grams
Fruit, dried	1 cup	4 ounces	120 grams
Fruits or veggies, chopped	1 cup	5 to 7 ounces	145 to 200 grams
Fruits or veggies, puréed	1 cup	8.5 ounces	245 grams
Honey, maple syrup, or corn syrup	1 tablespoon	.75 ounce	20 grams
Liquids: cream, milk, water, or juice	1 cup	8 fluid ounces	240 milliliters
Oats	1 cup	5.5 ounces	150 grams
Salt	1 teaspoon	0.2 ounce	6 grams
Spices: cinnamon, cloves, ginger, or nutmeg (ground)	1 teaspoon	0.2 ounce	5 milliliters
Sugar, brown, firmly packed	1 cup	7 ounces	200 grams
Sugar, white	1 cup/1 tablespoon	7 ounces/0.5 ounce	200 grams/12.5 grams
Vanilla extract	1 teaspoon	0.2 ounce	4 grams

Fahrenheit	Celsius	Gas Mark
225°	110°	$1/4$
250°	120°	$1/2$
275°	140°	1
300°	150°	2
325°	160°	3
350°	180°	4
375°	190°	5
400°	200°	6
425°	220°	7
450°	230°	8

Index

Italian Meatballs in Sauce, 95

Quinoa with Toasted Pine Nuts, 189